LITTLE BOOKS
ABOUT BIG THINGS

CLASSICAL
MYTHOLOGY

LITTLE BOOKS
ABOUT BIG
THINGS

CLASSICAL
MYTHOLOGY

BOB BAILEY MUCKER

FALL RIVER PRESS

New York

FALL RIVER PRESS

New York

An Imprint of Sterling Publishing
387 Park Avenue South
New York, NY 10016

Cover design by Igor Satanovsky

The information in this book has been drawn from multiple sources, and is
assumed to be accurate as printed. Although every effort has been made to verify
the information by source, the publisher cannot guarantee its perfect accuracy.

ISBN 978-1-4351-4683-9

Distributed in Canada by Sterling Publishing
c/o Canadian Manda Group, 165 Dufferin Street
Toronto, Ontario, Canada M6K 3H6
Distributed in the United Kingdom by GMC Distribution Services
Castle Place, 166 High Street, Lewes, East Sussex, England BN7 1XU
Distributed in Australia by Capricorn Link (Australia) Pty. Ltd.
P.O. Box 704, Windsor, NSW 2756, Australia

For information about custom editions, special sales, and premium and
corporate purchases, please contact Sterling Special Sales at 800-805-5489 or
specialsales@sterlingpublishing.com.

Printed in China

2 4 6 8 10 9 7 5 3 1

www.sterlingpublishing.com

G ods and goddesses are everywhere. This has nothing to do with your spiritual or religious beliefs. It's a plain fact.

There are gods and goddesses on our maps, in the words we speak, in the air we breathe, even in outer space. Among the legacies left us by ancient civilizations, you could say mythology has had the most pervasive and subtle influence on our lives. Most of us probably "interact" with gods and goddesses every day without even knowing we're doing it.

And then there are the stories: about good and evil, right and wrong, love and hate. Many of the books and movies and TV shows we enjoy take their plots directly from ancient mythological tales and beliefs. And why not? Those stories were intended to be something that ordinary people could understand and identify with. Mythology gives us life lessons.

Mythological tales are as old as civilization itself and trying to cover them all would be a Herculean task. (See? Herculean: from Hercules, the mythological hero.) This little book will focus on gods and goddesses who cross our paths in everyday life and the lessons they've been teaching people since ancient times—with a few wild and crazy tales to boot.

L ET'S BEGIN AT THE BEGINNING, with the creation of the world. Every mythology has a story about how things all got started: how the Earth was formed and how humans came to exist.

The most common creation story from Greek mythology (there are a couple) says that Earth was formed from Chaos. The word chaos means "void," or "abyss"—basically a whole lot of nothingness.

Somehow—and even the ancient poet Hesiod, who wrote the definitive history of these things doesn't say how—out of Chaos miraculously sprang Gaia, the Earth.

IF YOU'RE LOOKING FOR LIFE LESSONS in mythology (and we are) here's one: beautiful, wonderful things can come from what seems like a hopeless mess. After all, Earth came from nothing; and what could be more beautiful and wonderful than Earth?

But there's a downside…

—⟡—

CHAOS ALSO PRODUCED EREBUS (darkness) and Nyx (night). And even worse, Chaos produced Tartarus, the special place in the underworld where wicked people are sent to live in eternal torment. You have probably heard about some of them and the punishments they endured for the bad things they did to the gods or to their fellow mortals.

Mythological "Criminals" Sentenced to Eternal Torment

Ixion:
Patricide, Rape

Sisyphus:
Fraud, Embezzlement,
Insubordination, Parole Violation

Tantalus:
Theft, Perjury

EVEN IF YOU DON'T KNOW the story of Sisyphus, you've probably experienced it: the feeling that you keep doing the same job over and over and never seem to make any progress. Just when you think you're about to reach your goal, something forces you to go right back to where you started.

That was the eternal torment to which Sisyphus was sentenced. But unlike you, he really deserved it.

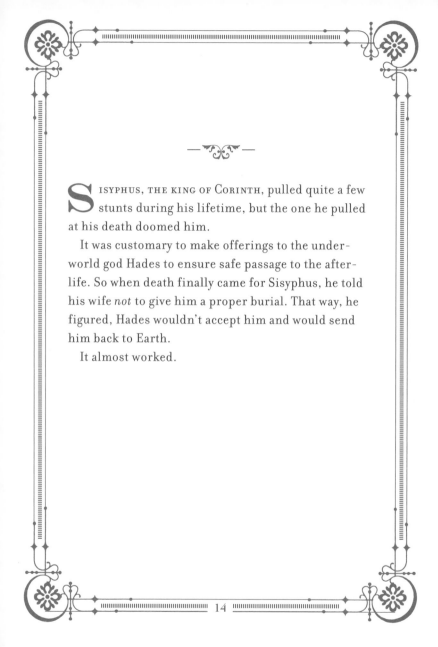

SISYPHUS, THE KING OF CORINTH, pulled quite a few stunts during his lifetime, but the one he pulled at his death doomed him.

It was customary to make offerings to the underworld god Hades to ensure safe passage to the afterlife. So when death finally came for Sisyphus, he told his wife *not* to give him a proper burial. That way, he figured, Hades wouldn't accept him and would send him back to Earth.

It almost worked.

Hades sent Sisyphus back to Earth with instructions to punish his wife for not doing what was proper. But once Sisyphus was home—and alive—he simply went on living as if he'd never died.

When he finally returned to the underworld (as everyone must), Sisyphus was sentenced to roll a boulder up a hill; but just as he approached the top, the boulder would roll back down. And Sisyphus had to start all over again. Every single day. For all eternity.

Magic Number 3

THE GODS WERE EXTREMELY SKILLED at punishing people for wrongdoing, but no one was as skilled as the three avenging spirits known in Greek as the Erinyes and in Latin as the Furies. They were Alecto (relentless or unceasing anger), Tisiphone (voice of revenge), and Megaera (grudge); but the ancient Greeks were so afraid to offend them they rarely mentioned them by name.

People sometimes called them the Eumenides—the kind ones—in sort of the same way you'd say "Nice doggie" to a snarling hound that's about to bite your leg off.

— ✦✦✦ —

*T*HE *EUMENIDES* BY THE GREEK PLAYWRIGHT Aeschylus (circa 458 BC) tells the story of Orestes who murdered his mother, Clytemnestra, because she had murdered his father (her husband) Agamemnon.

Acting on orders direct from the god Apollo, Orestes commits the revenge crime. But the Erinyes won't stand for that. They pursue Orestes and threaten to drive him mad (their usual method of punishing evil). They won't even listen to Apollo when he tells them to stop.

Only Athena, goddess of wisdom, can intercede to save Orestes. Like tossing a bone to that angry dog, Athena soothes the Erinyes with respect and veneration. "You're older and wiser than I am," she tells them. "What can I do to make you happy?"

They finally settle on giving the Erinyes power over which households will prosper and which will not.

And so the "angry ones" (Erinyes) become the "soothed ones" (Eumenides).

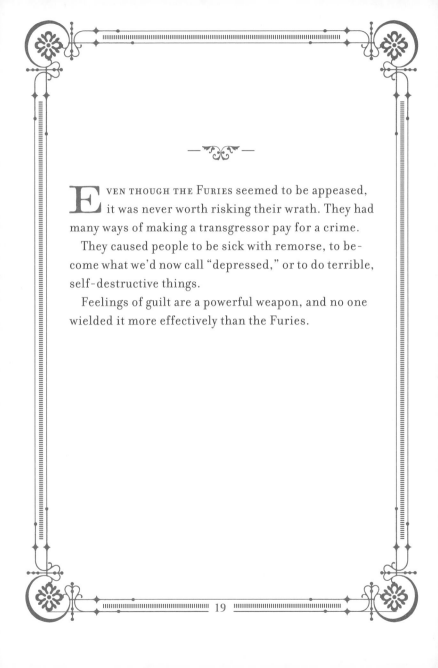

E VEN THOUGH THE FURIES seemed to be appeased, it was never worth risking their wrath. They had many ways of making a transgressor pay for a crime.

They caused people to be sick with remorse, to become what we'd now call "depressed," or to do terrible, self-destructive things.

Feelings of guilt are a powerful weapon, and no one wielded it more effectively than the Furies.

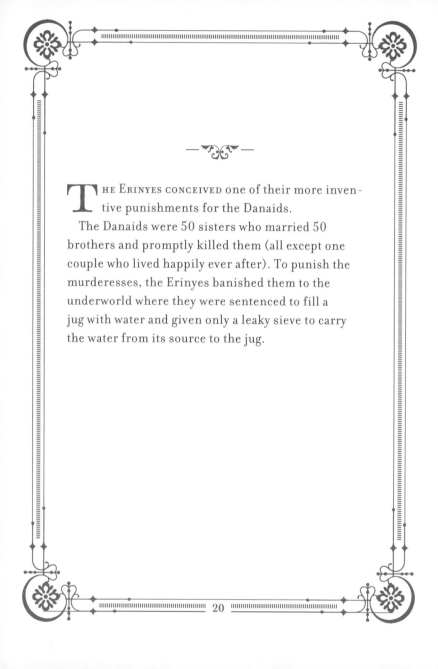

T HE ERINYES CONCEIVED one of their more inventive punishments for the Danaids.

The Danaids were 50 sisters who married 50 brothers and promptly killed them (all except one couple who lived happily ever after). To punish the murderesses, the Erinyes banished them to the underworld where they were sentenced to fill a jug with water and given only a leaky sieve to carry the water from its source to the jug.

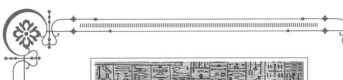

WHAT HAPPENS AFTER WE DIE? The ancients pondered that question as often as we do today.

If you were an ancient Egyptian you wanted to make sure the afterlife didn't include an encounter with Ammut—the eater of souls.

Head of a crocodile, body of a lioness, rear of a hippopotamus, Ammut was a female demon who took the last measure of a person's deeds. If he'd been wicked, Ammut would eat his soul and he'd spend eternity in torment.

*Was the mythological underworld always
a terrible place?*

Not at all. There were locations reserved for particularly
bad people. Tartarus, in Greek mythology, was one. Niflhel,
one of the nine regions of the Underworld in Norse
mythology, was another.

For honorable people, however, the underworld could
be swell. In Welsh mythology, Annwfn is a beautiful "other
world" of the afterlife. In Greek mythology, Elysium is
reserved for heroes and the righteous chosen by the
gods. In Norse mythology, Gimli is paradise. In Egyptian
mythology, good people joined the god Osiris in Sekhet-
hetepet, the Fields of Peace.

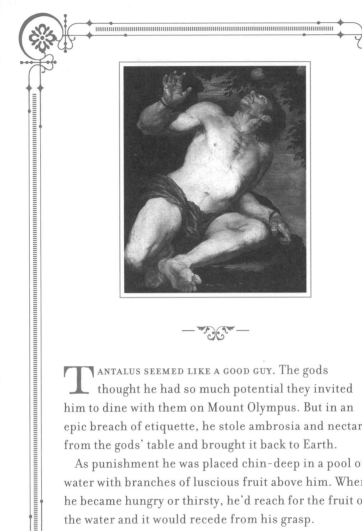

TANTALUS SEEMED LIKE A GOOD GUY. The gods thought he had so much potential they invited him to dine with them on Mount Olympus. But in an epic breach of etiquette, he stole ambrosia and nectar from the gods' table and brought it back to Earth.

As punishment he was placed chin-deep in a pool of water with branches of luscious fruit above him. When he became hungry or thirsty, he'd reach for the fruit or the water and it would recede from his grasp.

That's where we get the word "tantalizing."

Words of the Gods, Part I

1. A somnambulist…
   a. Laughs a lot   b. Builds houses   c. Walks in his sleep

2. Cereal takes its name from the Roman goddess of…
   a. Agriculture   b. Breakfast   c. Dawn

3. Martial arts are used in…
   a. Cooking   b. Combat   c. Public speaking

4. Someone with the Midas touch is successful at…
   a. Making money   b. Politics   c. Sports

5. A mnemonic is a trick that helps you…
   a. Find love   b. Lose weight   c. Remember things

ANSWERS

1. c. Somnus, Roman god of sleep, gave us the root for somnambulism, or sleep-walking.

2. a. Ceres, the Roman goddess of agriculture, brought wheat to mankind.

3. b. Martial arts are warlike, just like Mars, the Roman god of war.

4. a. Mythical King Midas asked the gods for the power to turn everything he touched to gold. Great idea; until he touched his beloved daughter and *she* turned to gold.

5. c. Mnemosyne is the Greek goddess of memory. A mnemonic helps you remember things, such as thinking of "Roy G. Biv" to recall red, orange, yellow, green, blue, indigo, violet—the colors of the spectrum.

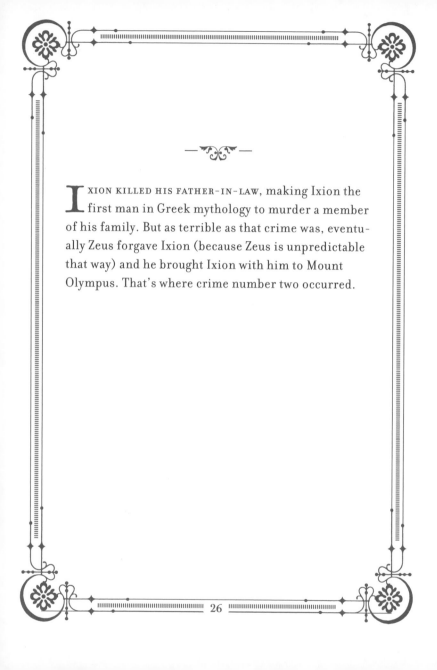

IXION KILLED HIS FATHER-IN-LAW, making Ixion the first man in Greek mythology to murder a member of his family. But as terrible as that crime was, eventually Zeus forgave Ixion (because Zeus is unpredictable that way) and he brought Ixion with him to Mount Olympus. That's where crime number two occurred.

I XION FELL IN LOVE with Hera, Zeus's wife, and tried to have his way with her. Hera told Zeus immediately and Zeus was none too pleased.

To test whether Hera's story was true, Zeus sculpted a fake Hera from clouds and tricked Ixion into seducing the cloud-Hera—which he happily did. This, of course, would have serious consequences.

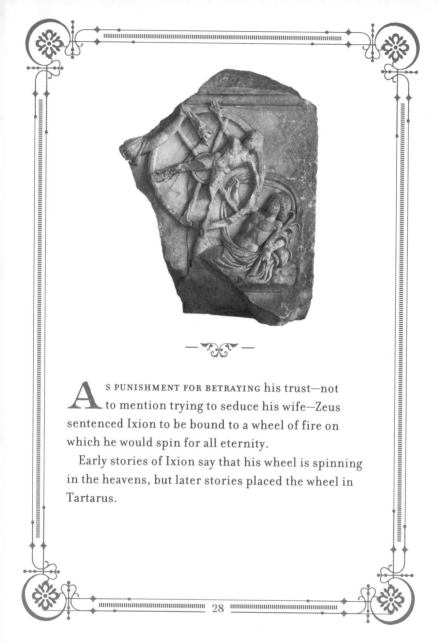

— ❧❀❧ —

A S PUNISHMENT FOR BETRAYING his trust—not to mention trying to seduce his wife—Zeus sentenced Ixion to be bound to a wheel of fire on which he would spin for all eternity.

Early stories of Ixion say that his wheel is spinning in the heavens, but later stories placed the wheel in Tartarus.

*What happened between Ixion
and the cloud-Hera?*

Besides ensuring that Ixion would be damned for all time, the unusual coupling between Ixion and the cloud-Hera had another result: cloud-Hera gave birth to Centaurus, who was not a beautiful or likeable creature.

Centaurus went to live in the mountains, where he found companionship among the Magnesian mares and together they created a race of centaurs—with the torso of a man and the body and legs of a horse.

— ❧ —

THE CENTAURS THAT DESCENDED from Centaurus were cruel, belligerent, and oversexed. They were trouble any way you looked at them. People feared them—or at least avoided them.

The exception was Chiron, a centaur with different bloodlines. He was the "child" of the Titan Cronus and the nymph Philyra, another unusual coupling.

CRONUS, WHO WAS MARRIED to the goddess Rhea, should not have been looking at other female deities. Nevertheless, like most gods, he had a wandering eye.

Cronus took a shine to Philyra, but to make sure Rhea didn't catch him in the act, he turned himself into a horse before he seduced Philyra. Lo and behold, the result of their coupling was a half man-half horse creature.

— ❧ —

PHILYRA WAS DISTRAUGHT when she saw her off-spring, but Chiron turned out to be the best of all centaurs. He was wise and gentle, and had a gift for music and for healing. He taught Asclepius, the Greek god of medicine, all he knew about surgery and medicines.

The god Apollo taught Chiron the art of archery, and Chiron passed that knowledge on to the heroes of Greek mythology, including Jason and Achilles. He even taught Heracles (also known as Hercules to the Romans), who—in an unfortunate accident— mortally wounded Chiron.

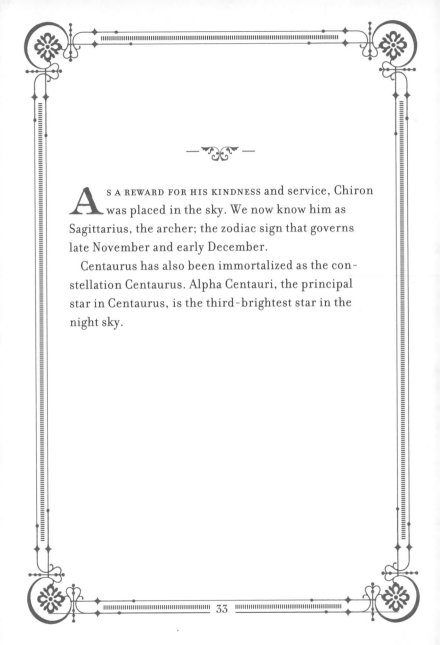

AS A REWARD FOR HIS KINDNESS and service, Chiron was placed in the sky. We now know him as Sagittarius, the archer; the zodiac sign that governs late November and early December.

Centaurus has also been immortalized as the constellation Centaurus. Alpha Centauri, the principal star in Centaurus, is the third-brightest star in the night sky.

Scholars who study the origin of myths (because mythology had to come from somewhere) love centaurs because their roots in the "real world" seem clear. An ancient or primitive person seeing a man on horseback for the first time could be forgiven for thinking that the man and the horse were actually one creature: human upper body and equine lower body.

Share those stories with a few of your fellow primitives, and soon a myth is born!

POP QUIZ

Mythological Interbreeding

1. In Greek mythology, Kampe is a she-dragon with the tail of a...
   a. Bird   b. Fish   c. Scorpion

2. Medusa, the Gorgon, had a head covered with...
   a. Blood   b. Frogs   c. Snakes

3. The Egyptian deities Ammut and Taweret both have characteristics of what animal?
   a. Camel   b. Chicken   c. Hippopotamus

4. The goat-legged god who guarded shepherds was known by what name in Greek mythology?
   a. Melampus   b. Pan   c. Tiberius

5. The ancient Greeks believed the Minotaur was half man and half...
   a. Bull   b. Falcon   c. Horse

ANSWERS

1. c. Kampe had the torso of a woman, the lower body of a dragon, vipers for feet, wings, and a scorpion's tail. She also shot sparks from her eyes. She guarded a pit in Tartarus until Zeus killed her.

2. c. When the Greek hero Perseus cut off Medusa's snake-covered head, the winged horse Pegasus popped out.

3. c. Egyptians admired the strength of the hippo; Ammut and Taweret had hippo traits.

4. b. Pan was the troublemaking, goat-legged Greek god of shepherds and sheep. The word "panic" comes from his name.

5. a. The Minotaur was conceived by Queen Pasiphae who disguised herself as a cow to mate with a bull.

Magic Number 7 + 7

KING MINOS OF CRETE was not at all pleased when his wife, Pasiphae, mated with a bull to give birth to the Minotaur—who had a bull's head and tail and a man's body. Minos imprisoned the Minotaur in a labyrinth and fed him with seven young men and seven virgins who were supplied from Athens every nine years.

Why is Ekhidna called the "Mother of Monsters"?

With a pretty nymph's face, flashing black eyes, and the body of a dragon, Ekhidna was destined to breed trouble. Among her offspring were:

- the Chimera, a fire-breathing goat/lion/snake creature;
- the Sphinx;
- the three-headed hell hound Cerberus and his two-headed brother Orthrus;
- the Hydra, a nine-headed water serpent; and
- the Caucasian Eagle sent by Zeus to peck out the liver of Prometheus.

Mythological Beasts

Basilisk: Serpent that kills with a touch

Calydonian Boar: Sent by Artemis to wreak havoc
on those who didn't pay her proper respect

Karkinos: Giant crab killed along
with the Hydra by Hercules

Kraken: Sea creature like a giant squid
from Norse mythology

Laelaps: Magical hound able to catch everything it hunted

Manticore: Body of a lion, face of a man,
and a spiky tail that shoots arrows

Ophiotauros: Half bull, half serpent

Teumessian Fox: Preyed upon the children of Thebes

WHEN LAELAPS WAS BROUGHT IN to catch the Teumessian Fox it presented a conundrum. The Teumessian Fox was "uncatchable" and Laelaps was "inescapable." Neither could expect to triumph in this showdown and they seemed destined to chase each other forever.

So Zeus, in his wisdom, decided to put a stop to the unwinnable contest. Depending on the story, he either turned them both to stone or placed them in the heavens as the constellations Canis Major and Canis Minor—the big and little dogs.

— ✦ —

THE ANCIENTS KNEW THE BASICS of how babies are made. If they didn't none of us would be here today. Still, they had some interesting myths about how human beings first appeared in the world. The most common Greek myth says that Prometheus created humans by molding them out of clay.

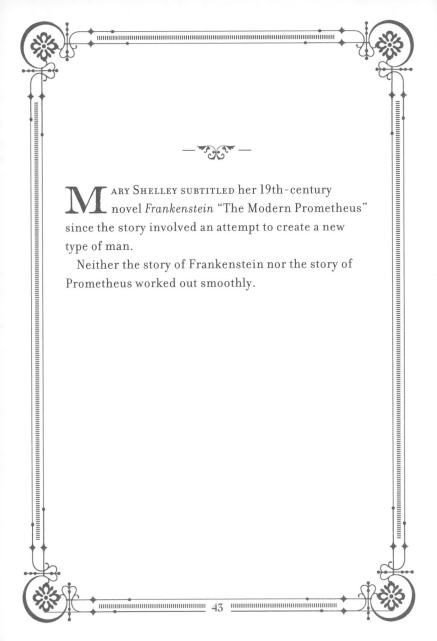

Mary Shelley subtitled her 19th-century novel *Frankenstein* "The Modern Prometheus" since the story involved an attempt to create a new type of man.

Neither the story of Frankenstein nor the story of Prometheus worked out smoothly.

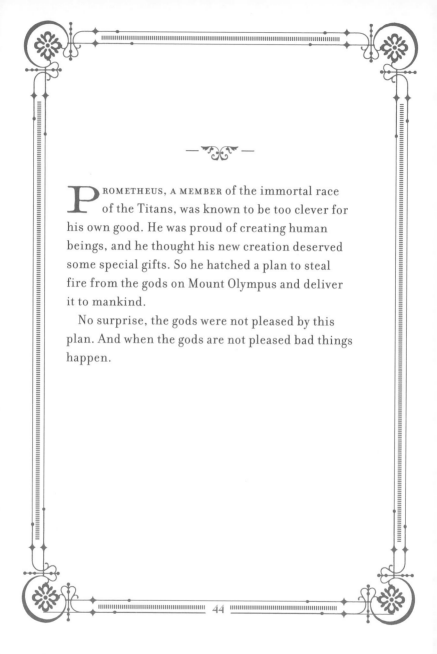

Prometheus, a member of the immortal race of the Titans, was known to be too clever for his own good. He was proud of creating human beings, and he thought his new creation deserved some special gifts. So he hatched a plan to steal fire from the gods on Mount Olympus and deliver it to mankind.

No surprise, the gods were not pleased by this plan. And when the gods are not pleased bad things happen.

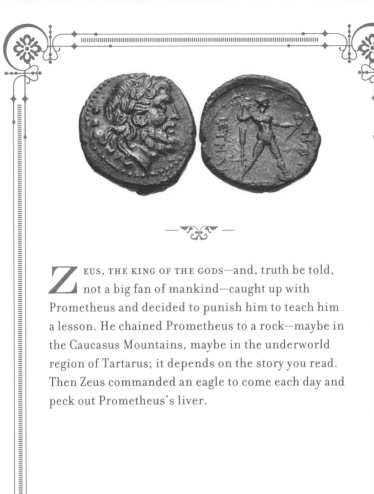

Z EUS, THE KING OF THE GODS—and, truth be told,
not a big fan of mankind—caught up with
Prometheus and decided to punish him to teach him
a lesson. He chained Prometheus to a rock—maybe in
the Caucasus Mountains, maybe in the underworld
region of Tartarus; it depends on the story you read.
Then Zeus commanded an eagle to come each day and
peck out Prometheus's liver.

—❧❦❧—

BECAUSE PROMETHEUS WAS IMMORTAL, his liver would grow back every night. Then every morning, the eagle would return and peck it out again.

Eventually Hercules was allowed to rescue Prometheus, who presumably had learned his lesson by then.

But Zeus wasn't finished with tormenting Prometheus…or mankind.

S INCE MAN HAD ACQUIRED FIRE without Zeus's permission (thanks to Prometheus) Zeus decided to take something away from him as compensation.

So he came up with the idea of Pandora, the first woman on Earth. Her job, as Zeus saw it, was to wreak havoc on mankind. She turned out to be very effective.

I F ZEUS HAD A WEAKNESS, it was his inability to control his desires. Place a beautiful creature before him and he'd do anything to have it. Greek mythology is filled with tales of Zeus's relentless pursuits of all manner of being.

He knew others shared his weakness, so he designed an irresistibly desirable woman and instructed Hephaestus to make her out of clay and water. Then Zeus gave her a secret weapon.

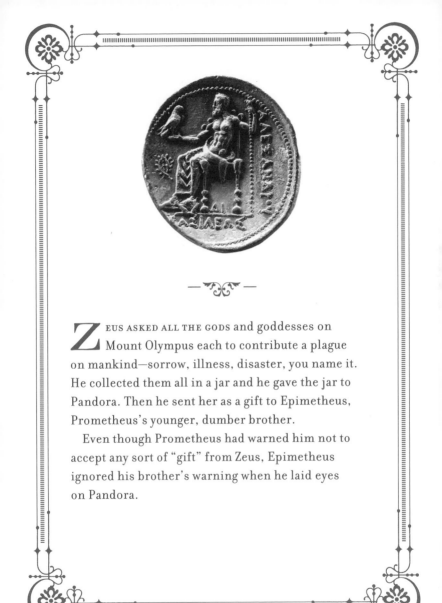

Z EUS ASKED ALL THE GODS and goddesses on
Mount Olympus each to contribute a plague
on mankind—sorrow, illness, disaster, you name it.
He collected them all in a jar and he gave the jar to
Pandora. Then he sent her as a gift to Epimetheus,
Prometheus's younger, dumber brother.

Even though Prometheus had warned him not to
accept any sort of "gift" from Zeus, Epimetheus
ignored his brother's warning when he laid eyes
on Pandora.

ONCE SHE WAS ENSCONCED on Earth, Pandora lifted the lid on that troublesome jar and let all the evils out to plague the world. (In the original myth it was a jar, not a box.)

Today people talk about a potentially problematic situation as a Pandora's Box. Once you lift the lid, you just don't know what's liable to come out.

What was in Pandora's Box?

All the evils of the world were in Pandora's Box—everything that makes humans miserable. But there are many interpretations of the Pandora myth and some are a little kinder. Pandora's name means "all gifts," which some stories say means that she brought both bad and good to Earth.

The problem was, when she opened the jar of good gifts, they all flew away.

Magic Number 12

THERE ARE LOTS and lots of gods in Greek mythology, and that doesn't even include the myriad immortal, magical, and semi-divine beings and creatures that populate the myths. But when it comes to the biggies—the ones who make it all happen—there are 12 gods and goddesses known as Olympians because they live on Olympus, the gods' headquarters.

Aphrodite (love)
Apollo (prophecy)
Ares (war)
Artemis (hunting)
Athena (wisdom)
Demeter (agriculture)
Dionysus (wine)
Hephaestus (fire)
Hera (wife of Zeus)
Hermes (messenger god)
Poseidon (sea)
Zeus (sky)

POP QUIZ

Miracle Births

1. Juno gave birth to Mars, the Roman god of war, after she was impregnated by a...
   a. Bull   b. Flower   c. Wolf

2. Who sprang to life, fully formed, from the head of Zeus?
   a. Athena   b. Medusa   c. Odysseus

3. Dionysus, Greek god of wine, came from...
   a. A grapevine   b. A stalk of wheat   c. Zeus's thigh

4. Hephaestus, Greek god of fire and the forge, had no father. His mother was...
   a. Gaia   b. Hera   c. Persephone

5. Adonis, the most handsome man on Earth, was born from a...
   a. Peacock   b. Sunrise   c. Tree

ANSWERS

1. b. Juno was angry when her husband, Jupiter, produced
   Minerva from his head without Juno's help. Flora,
   goddess of plants and flowers, touched Juno with a
   magic flower and Mars was conceived.

2. a. Athena, Greek goddess of wisdom, came from the
   head of Zeus. Minerva, the Roman goddess of wisdom,
   came from the head of Jupiter. See the answer above
   for more on that story!

3. c. When Dionysus's mother miscarried, Zeus pitched
   in as a divine incubator.

4. b. Poor Hephaestus! When Hera saw that he was born
   with a limp, she threw him out of Olympus and into the
   sea. The kind nymphs Thetis and Eurynome raised him.

5. c. Adonis was born from a myrrh tree. Read on to find
   out how.

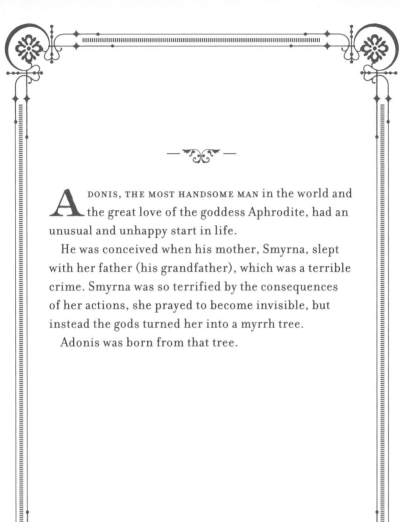

ADONIS, THE MOST HANDSOME MAN in the world and the great love of the goddess Aphrodite, had an unusual and unhappy start in life.

He was conceived when his mother, Smyrna, slept with her father (his grandfather), which was a terrible crime. Smyrna was so terrified by the consequences of her actions, she prayed to become invisible, but instead the gods turned her into a myrrh tree.

Adonis was born from that tree.

MYRRH RESIN WAS A VERSATILE and valuable item in ancient times. Ancient Egyptians used it to embalm bodies for mummification. The New Testament tells us it was also one of the three gifts—along with gold and frankincense—brought by the three Wise Men to the baby Jesus in the manger.

THE MOST FAMOUS "MIRACLE BIRTH" in Greek mythology is that of Athena, goddess of wisdom, who sprang fully formed from the head of Zeus.

Athena did have a mother; she was Metis, a Titaness, whose name means "wise counsel." Metis was wise, but she had a fatal weakness: she trusted Zeus. They married and she became pregnant, but when it was prophesied that the child would be smarter than Zeus, he swallowed Metis whole to prevent her from giving birth. Ultimately, this led to her death, and allowed Zeus to absorb all her wisdom!

NOT ONE TO BE DENIED, Athena poked and prodded the inside of Zeus's skull, causing him such a headache that he found someone—either Hephaestus or Prometheus, depending on who's telling the story—to split open his head and relieve the pain.

Some stories say Athena, also the goddess of military strategy, was born wearing full military armor. She used her spear to drive Zeus mad with pain until he let her out.

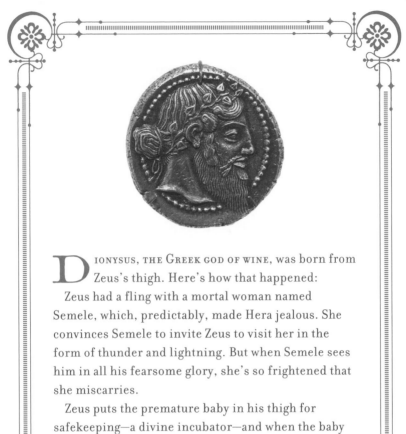

Dionysus, the Greek god of wine, was born from Zeus's thigh. Here's how that happened:

Zeus had a fling with a mortal woman named Semele, which, predictably, made Hera jealous. She convinces Semele to invite Zeus to visit her in the form of thunder and lightning. But when Semele sees him in all his fearsome glory, she's so frightened that she miscarries.

Zeus puts the premature baby in his thigh for safekeeping—a divine incubator—and when the baby is born, he's Dionysus.

HEPHAESTUS

— ❧ —

E VEN THOUGH ZEUS IS the immortal poster boy for behaving badly, his wife, Hera, isn't exactly an innocent. She gave birth to Hephaestus, the god of fire, metallurgy, and masonry, without help from a consort—or so one story goes.

The common myth says that Hera was so angry at Zeus for giving birth to Athena, she contrived to give birth on her own and that child was Hephaestus. Chronologically, that would make it impossible for Hephaestus to be the one who split open Zeus's head to let Athena out. But let's not quibble over details with the gods.

Magic Number 50

— ❦ —

THAT'S AN ESTIMATE of the number of children Zeus fathered based on common myths, but the details of some are conflicting or unclear. That figure also doesn't include the dozens of mortals who claimed to be descended from Zeus. (Kings and other nobles always liked to tell people they inherited their positions directly from the gods.)

Of all those children, Zeus had only three with his wife/sister Hera: Ares, the god of war; Eileithyia, goddess of childbirth; and Hebe, goddess of youth.

HEBE

Mythological Children Who Disobeyed Their Parents

Icarus

His father, Daedalus, made wings of wax so they could fly from captivity to freedom. Even though he was warned not to, Icarus flew too close to the sun. The wax wings melted and he fell to his death.

Persephone

Her mom, Demeter, told her not to wander off by herself. When she did, Persephone was kidnapped by Hades and forced to marry him and live in the underworld.

Phaeton

Took his dad's fiery chariot of the sun out for a spin and ended up in a terrible crash.

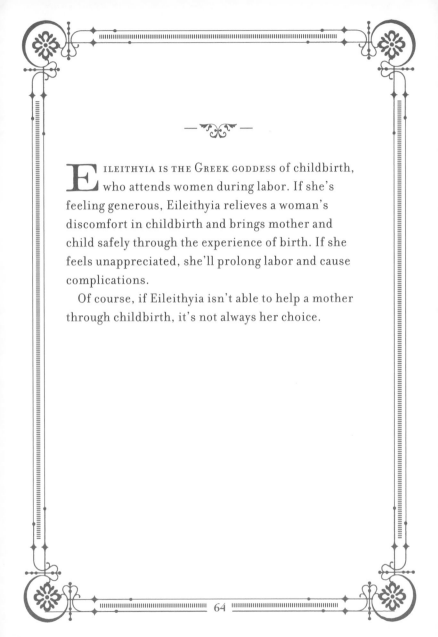

EILEITHYIA IS THE GREEK GODDESS of childbirth, who attends women during labor. If she's feeling generous, Eileithyia relieves a woman's discomfort in childbirth and brings mother and child safely through the experience of birth. If she feels unappreciated, she'll prolong labor and cause complications.

Of course, if Eileithyia isn't able to help a mother through childbirth, it's not always her choice.

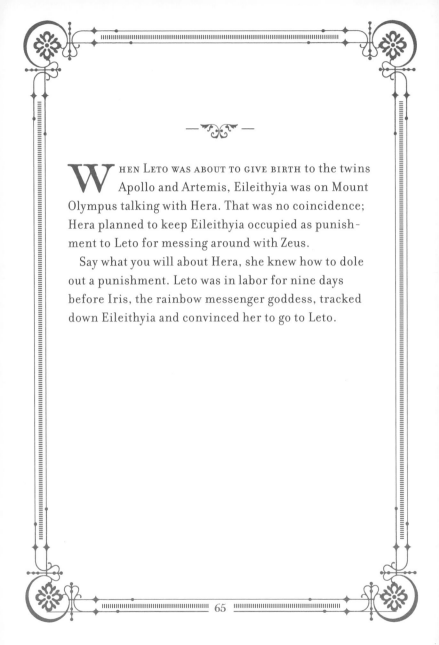

WHEN LETO WAS ABOUT TO GIVE BIRTH to the twins Apollo and Artemis, Eileithyia was on Mount Olympus talking with Hera. That was no coincidence; Hera planned to keep Eileithyia occupied as punishment to Leto for messing around with Zeus.

Say what you will about Hera, she knew how to dole out a punishment. Leto was in labor for nine days before Iris, the rainbow messenger goddess, tracked down Eileithyia and convinced her to go to Leto.

ARCHAEOLOGISTS HAVE FOUND many shrines to Eileithyia filled with offerings, tiny statues, and traces of ancient incense burned in her honor.

Although scholars don't agree on the meaning of her name, some loosely translate Eileithyia as "deliverer" based on the Greek word for "freedom."

Statues of the goddess sometimes show her in a kneeling position—the same position women would assume to ease their pain when they were about to give birth.

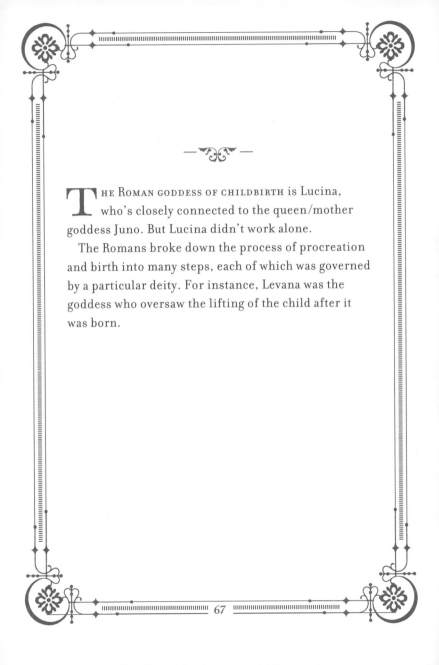

THE ROMAN GODDESS OF CHILDBIRTH is Lucina, who's closely connected to the queen/mother goddess Juno. But Lucina didn't work alone.

The Romans broke down the process of procreation and birth into many steps, each of which was governed by a particular deity. For instance, Levana was the goddess who oversaw the lifting of the child after it was born.

C ARMENTA WAS ANOTHER ROMAN DEITY connected to childbirth. Each January, according to the poet Ovid, women celebrated a festival known as Carmentalia in her honor. She was a seer, and a patron of midwives, and—for some reason that's not clear— she's also credited with converting the Greek alphabet into the Latin alphabet.

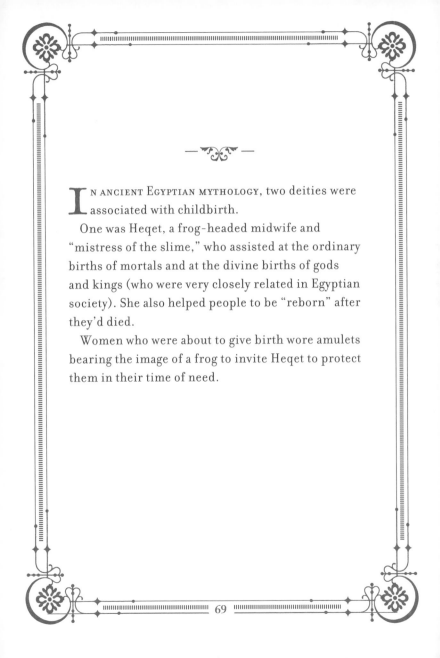

—⁓⁎⁓—

IN ANCIENT EGYPTIAN MYTHOLOGY, two deities were associated with childbirth.

One was Heqet, a frog-headed midwife and "mistress of the slime," who assisted at the ordinary births of mortals and at the divine births of gods and kings (who were very closely related in Egyptian society). She also helped people to be "reborn" after they'd died.

Women who were about to give birth wore amulets bearing the image of a frog to invite Heqet to protect them in their time of need.

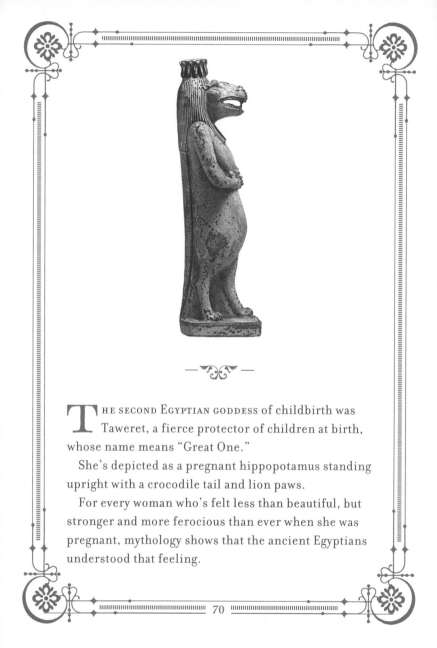

— ✦ —

THE SECOND EGYPTIAN GODDESS of childbirth was
Taweret, a fierce protector of children at birth,
whose name means "Great One."

She's depicted as a pregnant hippopotamus standing
upright with a crocodile tail and lion paws.

For every woman who's felt less than beautiful, but
stronger and more ferocious than ever when she was
pregnant, mythology shows that the ancient Egyptians
understood that feeling.

—✦🙟🙝✦—

IN GREEK MYTHOLOGY, after Leto gave birth to Artemis, the goddess of the hunt, Artemis immediately helped with the delivery of her twin brother Apollo.

Artemis has been closely linked to childbirth and to Eileithyia ever since, and she's given big sisters who "help" with their little brothers a high standard to live up to.

Mythological Twins

Apollo and Artemis
The children of Zeus and Leto didn't always get along, but they teamed up to defend their mother's honor.

Castor and Pollux
When Castor was killed, Pollux gave up his immortality to be with him forever.

Romulus and Remus
They founded their own city, but quarreled over who would rule it. Romulus killed Remus and named the city for himself: Rome.

Geb and Nut
These brother-sister Egyptian twins married and produced twins Osiris and Isis, who also married.

Freyr and Freyja
The beautiful brother-sister twins share responsibility for fertility in Norse mythology.

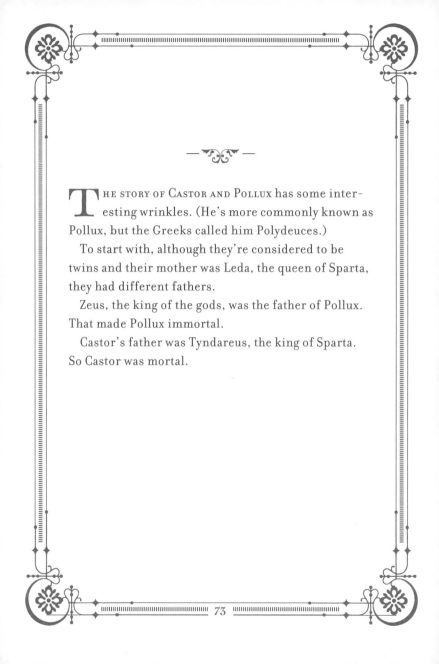

THE STORY OF CASTOR AND POLLUX has some interesting wrinkles. (He's more commonly known as Pollux, but the Greeks called him Polydeuces.)

To start with, although they're considered to be twins and their mother was Leda, the queen of Sparta, they had different fathers.

Zeus, the king of the gods, was the father of Pollux. That made Pollux immortal.

Castor's father was Tyndareus, the king of Sparta. So Castor was mortal.

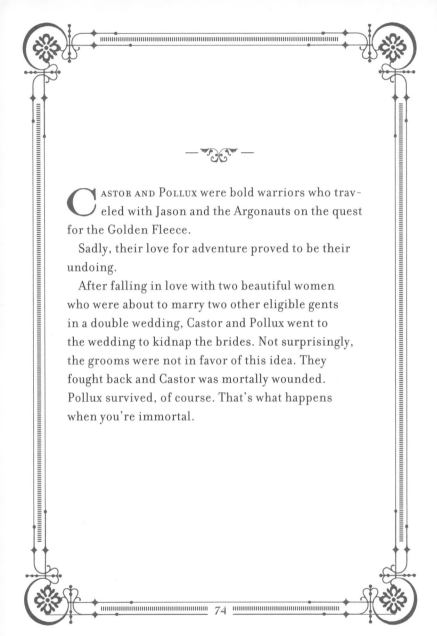

CASTOR AND POLLUX were bold warriors who traveled with Jason and the Argonauts on the quest for the Golden Fleece.

Sadly, their love for adventure proved to be their undoing.

After falling in love with two beautiful women who were about to marry two other eligible gents in a double wedding, Castor and Pollux went to the wedding to kidnap the brides. Not surprisingly, the grooms were not in favor of this idea. They fought back and Castor was mortally wounded. Pollux survived, of course. That's what happens when you're immortal.

— ✤ —

W HEN CASTOR DIED, Pollux begged Zeus to let him join his brother in the afterlife.

Instead, Zeus sent Castor and Pollux to take up permanent residence together in the sky.

The two brightest stars in the constellation Gemini, also known as The Twins, are an orange giant called Pollux and a white triple star called Castor.

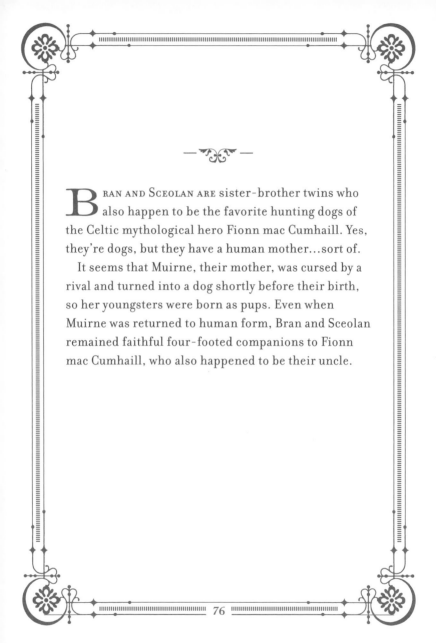

BRAN AND SCEOLAN ARE sister-brother twins who also happen to be the favorite hunting dogs of the Celtic mythological hero Fionn mac Cumhaill. Yes, they're dogs, but they have a human mother...sort of.

It seems that Muirne, their mother, was cursed by a rival and turned into a dog shortly before their birth, so her youngsters were born as pups. Even when Muirne was returned to human form, Bran and Sceolan remained faithful four-footed companions to Fionn mac Cumhaill, who also happened to be their uncle.

Parents Who Ate Their Children

Cronus
Ate five of his kids on purpose

Tereus
His angry wife served up the kid
as a dinner surprise

Thyestes
Mess with your brother's wife
and dine at your peril

Zeus
Gobbled up Athena
and her mother

WANT TO HIT AN ADULTERER where he lives? Kill his kids and serve them to him for supper. (Note: This is not recommended for mortals.)

Tereus raped Procne, his sister-in-law. So, Philomela, his wife, killed their son Itys. Then she and Procne cooked the boy for Tereus's supper.

Thyestes seduced the wife of his brother Atreus, so Atreus paid him back by cooking Thyestes's children and serving them to him in a stew.

CRONUS, KING OF THE TITANS, was a different case. A prophecy foretold that one of his children would depose him (as he had done to his father, Uranus), so Cronus swallowed his children…all except Zeus, whom Rhea managed to hide. Later, Zeus deposed Cronus—and forced him to vomit up the rest of the family.

How big were the Titans?

We use the word "titanic" to mean gigantic, but the Titans in Greek mythology weren't merely large, they were enormously powerful. What other race could give birth to the gods?

The birth of the Olympian gods meant the end of the Titans' reign. After Zeus made his father regurgitate the family, he started a war with Cronus that lasted ten years.

Magic Number 6

CRONUS AND RHEA—rulers of the Titans, husband and wife, and brother and sister—had six children:

Demeter

goddess of agriculture

Hades

god of the underworld

Hera

goddess of the heavens

Hestia

goddess of hearth and home

Poseidon

god of the sea

Zeus

god of the heavens

*Was it okay for gods and goddesses to marry
when they were brother and sister?*

The rules of mankind generally don't apply to immortals. Gods and goddesses married who they wanted, and had flings with who they wanted (in whatever form they wanted). This sort of thing was forbidden—or at least frowned upon—among mortals.

Mortal kings and queens were an exception, however, since they believed they were descended directly from the gods. Cleopatra's first husband was her younger brother Ptolemy XIII. After he died, her second husband was Ptolemy XIV, her even younger brother.

O F ALL THE BROTHER-SISTER/HUSBAND-WIFE pairs,
Zeus and Hera were the most famous and the
most tempestuous. They fought all the time, cheated
on each other regularly, and set the bar as high as
it could possibly be for power couples behaving badly.

Among the goddesses Zeus seduced was Demeter,
his sister and Hera's sister as well. Zeus and Demeter
mated when they were both in the form of snakes.
Appropriate.

A FTER THEIR COUPLING, Demeter gave birth to Persephone, a very beautiful and innocent goddess. To make sure she stayed that way, Demeter hid Persephone on an island for safekeeping. But Hades, god of the underworld, managed to find her and kidnap her.

If you're keeping track, you know that Hades is the brother of Zeus, Demeter, and Hera; and therefore Persephone's "double uncle." You also know this is not going to end well.

WITH SWEET PERSEPHONE in the underworld, Demeter went mad with worry and everything on Earth began to die. Rivers dried up. Plants withered. Animals became barren.

Things were so bad, even selfish Zeus took notice and interceded. He struck a deal with brother Hades: Persephone would spend half the year as his consort in the underworld and the other half spreading light and life on Earth.

This is why Persephone is associated with spring—the season in which the Earth comes back to life.

How is Proserpina related to Persephone?

Proserpina is the Roman counterpart to Persephone. Their stories are essentially the same, but in Roman mythology it's expressly stated that Proserpina was hidden on the island of Sicily, where she was tutored by Minerva, the goddess of wisdom, and Diana, the goddess of the hunt.

Persephone's Flowers

WHEN HADES KIDNAPPED HER, Persephone was picking flowers. According to a poem written by Homer, these were in her bouquet:

Crocus

Hyacinth

Iris

Lily

Narcissus

Rose

THE BRIGHTLY COLORED ANEMONE is sometimes called a windflower because the slightest wind will blow its petals away, and its name comes from the Greek for "daughter of the wind."

Red anemones are sacred to Aphrodite. It's said that she created them from the blood of her love, Adonis, after he died.

ELIOTROPE, A FLOWER THAT TURNS its face to follow the sun, takes its name from Helios the sun god. Klytie, a sea nymph loved him desperately, and he loved her too—for a while. When he eventually left her for another nymph, poor little Klytie wasted away until she became a flower that follows the sun.

— ❧ —

THE CROCUS TAKES ITS NAME from a mortal youth
name Krokos, a favorite of the god Hermes.
It seems that Hermes accidentally killed Krokos
by hitting him with a discus. The god was so upset
by what he'd done that he transformed the boy into
a lovely blue flower. At least that's one version of
the story.

— ❧ —

A SEPARATE, BUT SIMILAR STORY involves the god Apollo who accidentally killed a boy named Hyakinthos with a discus. That story goes on to explain that Apollo turned the boy into the flower we now know as hyacinth.

Scholars have studied and debated these tales to determine which is true. The only thing we can take from them is the message that throwing a discus at someone can be very, very dangerous. That's a lesson no one can dispute.

Who were the Lotus-eaters?

Either the happiest people on Earth or an object lesson about the dangers of addiction. In *The Odyssey*, the epic Greek poem by Homer, the hero, Odysseus, and his crew survive a storm at sea and arrive in a place where everyone subsists on the fruit and flowers of the lotus tree. It's delicious, but it's also narcotic, causing them to drift into an intoxicated state.

Odysseus stages the ancient version of an intervention to corral his men back onto the ship and away from the tempting lotus.

SOME STORIES SAY THAT the Lotus tree is named for the freshwater nymph Lotis, who turned into the tree when she was running away from the amorous advances of the fertility god Priapus.

Priapus was born to be bad. His parents were Dionysus, the god of wine, and Aphrodite, the goddess of love. We don't need to discuss the trouble that combination can cause!

PRIAPUS WAS A LECHER who took his role as the guardian of fruitfulness a bit too literally. Females weren't safe around him, and if you had any doubts about his intentions, the many depictions of him with grossly oversized genitals will make them obvious.

Ancient Greeks and Romans put statues of Priapus in their fields and gardens to increase fertility… and to chase birds away. Priapus was the world's first scarecrow!

THE NYMPHAEA, WHICH WE USUALLY call a water lily even though it's not related to the lily plant, was named for the mythological race of sweet young things known as nymphs. They lived in and around lakes and rivers and springs, so it was only natural to name a delicate water flower for them.

What's a nymph?

The easy answer is: a nymph is a female nature spirit, not mortal but not quite a full-fledged goddess. Nymphs are everywhere. They cluster in groups around water, in forests and fields…anywhere natural and beautiful. There also were a few nymphs that lived in the underworld.

Imagine that you're in the forest by a brook. The leaves flutter in the breeze. The water trickles over the stones. Everything seems alive. The ancients took that as evidence that nymphs were all around them.

Magic Number 50

— ❧ —

NYMPHS FIGURE IN SO MANY Greek and Roman myths because there were so many nymphs. There were 50 Nereids, or Sea Nymphs, alone. Their parents were Nereus and Doris, deities of the sea (most likely the Mediterranean) whose responsibilities included determining which fishermen would bring home bountiful catches.

The Nereids were patron spirits of sailors, who whispered kind, loving words about them to ensure that they would stay safe at sea.

POP QUIZ

The Mythological Universe

1. Nereid, Naiad, and Triton are satellites, or moons, of what planet?
   a. Neptune   b. Uranus   c. Venus

2. Scorpius was a deadly scorpion that battled what mythological hunter?
   a. Artemis   b. Britomartis   c. Orion

3. Titan is...
   a. a galaxy   b. the largest satellite/moon of Saturn
   c. a star in the constellation Leo

4. The constellations Leo, Cancer, and Hydra represent beasts slain by what hero?
   a. Achilles   b. Hercules   c. Odysseus

5. The Greek scholar Plutarch wrote about caverns on the moon named for...
   a. Eos   b. Hecate   c. Psyche

ANSWERS

1. a. Nereids and Naiads are water nymphs; Triton was a minor sea god who's usually depicted as a merman. Naturally, they orbit Neptune, the planet named for the Roman god of the sea.

2. c. Stories about Orion's battle with Scorpius vary (some say Scorpius killed Orion), but it was believed that after the fight Zeus placed them both in the sky as constellations.

3. b. Named for Titans, who were huge and powerful, the largest moon of the planet Saturn was first cataloged in 1655.

4. b. Leo the Lion, Cancer the Crab, and Hydra the Sea Monster were slain by Hercules.

5. b. The sorceress goddess Hecate was associated with the moon and the afterlife. The lunar crater that today's astronomers call Mare Imbrium—Sea of Showers—was once called the Caverns of Hecate, where souls went on their way to the underworld.

Some Elements Named for Mythological Figures

Cerium: Ceres, Roman goddess of agriculture

Helium: Helios, Greek god of the Sun

Iridium: Iris, Greek goddess of the rainbow

Mercury: Mercury, the Roman messenger of the gods

Titanium: The race of proto-gods known as the Titans

Selenium: Selene, a Greek moon goddess

Niobium: Niobe, Daughter of Tantalus and wife of Amphion of Thebes

Tellurium: Tellus, the Roman "Mother Earth" goddess similar to the Greek Gaia

Tantalum: Tantalus, the Phrygian king forever tantalized in Tartarus

Thorium: Thor, Norse god of thunder

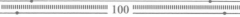

What does Helios have to do with helium?

Helium was first identified by observation during a solar eclipse in 1868 and for several years it was believed that helium only existed on the Sun. Several physicists, working independently in different countries but around the same time, contributed to the "discovery" of helium. English astronomer Joseph Norman Lockyer named the element in honor of the Greek god of the Sun.

E UROPIUM WAS NAMED for the continent of Europe, but the continent of Europe is (usually) thought to have been named for Europa, a Phoenician princess whom Zeus took a fancy to, turned himself into a bull, and had his way with her. (This is the sanitized version of the story.)

The story continues with Zeus (or Jupiter in the Roman version) kidnapping Europa and whisking her off to Crete, thereby taking the Middle Eastern princess—Phoenicia was located in what is now modern-day Lebanon—to "Europe."

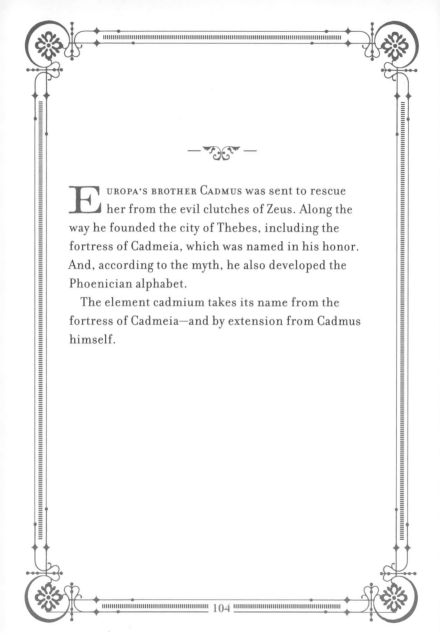

EUROPA'S BROTHER CADMUS was sent to rescue
her from the evil clutches of Zeus. Along the
way he founded the city of Thebes, including the
fortress of Cadmeia, which was named in his honor.
And, according to the myth, he also developed the
Phoenician alphabet.

The element cadmium takes its name from the
fortress of Cadmeia—and by extension from Cadmus
himself.

T HE ELEMENT COBALT takes its name from a
German myth about *kobold*, evil goblins that
haunt mines and cause trouble for miners by leaking
toxic gas (such as arsenic) into the air.

Nickel is also named for a deceitful German spirit
who haunted mines and fooled miners into thinking
they'd found a rich vein, when they hadn't. Miners
knew nickel well; they dug it up in copper mines, and
it looked very much like copper, but it was consider-
ably less valuable.

MERCURY'S GREEK COUNTERPART was Hermes, a versatile fellow. His primary job was messenger of the gods—he delivered gifts and packages, he carried messages and helped gods arrange secret romantic trysts, he even escorted souls to the underworld.

Hermes was so precocious it's said he was born in the morning and was walking by afternoon. He's been on the move ever since.

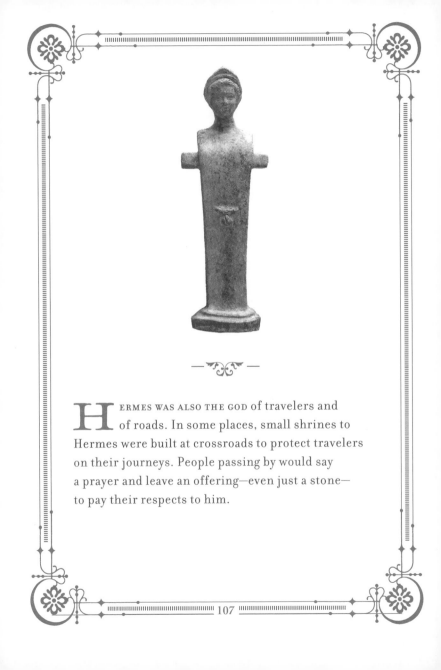

HERMES WAS ALSO THE GOD of travelers and of roads. In some places, small shrines to Hermes were built at crossroads to protect travelers on their journeys. People passing by would say a prayer and leave an offering—even just a stone— to pay their respects to him.

How the Gods Travel

Ares, the Greek god of war, drives a chariot drawn
by four immortal, fire-breathing horses.

Freya, the Norse goddess of fertility,
travels in a chariot drawn by two cats.

Freyr, the Norse god of fertility and favorable weather,
rides Gullinbursti, a boar with bristles made of gold.

Hera, the Greek queen of the gods,
rides in a chariot drawn by peacocks.

Medea flies in a chariot pulled by winged dragons.

Poseidon, the Greek god of the sea, has a chariot
drawn by fish-tailed horses, or hippocampi.

Rhea, the mother of the Greek gods,
drives a chariot drawn by lions.

Thor, the Norse thunder god,
rides in a chariot drawn by goats.

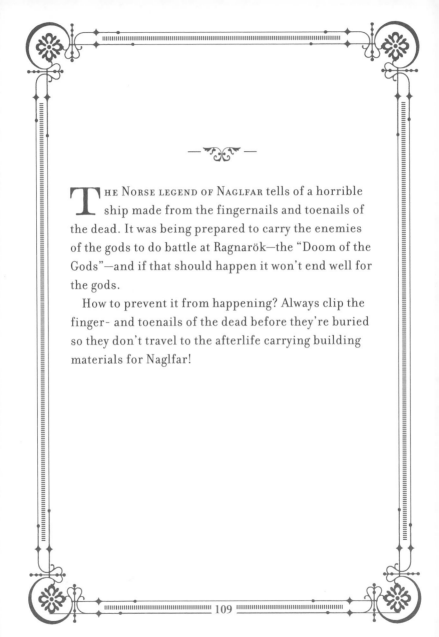

THE NORSE LEGEND OF NAGLFAR tells of a horrible ship made from the fingernails and toenails of the dead. It was being prepared to carry the enemies of the gods to do battle at Ragnarök—the "Doom of the Gods"—and if that should happen it won't end well for the gods.

How to prevent it from happening? Always clip the finger- and toenails of the dead before they're buried so they don't travel to the afterlife carrying building materials for Naglfar!

—❧❧❧—

THE ANCIENTS EXPLAINED the movement of the sun, from sunrise to sunset, through the story of Helios, the god of the sun. Every day, Helios drove his chariot of the sun across the sky, pulled by a team of fiery horses.

Although Helios and Apollo were both connected to the sun, and their stories sometimes overlap, they were separate beings. Helios was the son of the Titan Hyperion. Apollo was the son of Zeus.

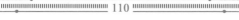

What happened when Phaeton
borrowed his dad's chariot?

Every parent who's ever lent his teenager the keys to the family car can identify with the story of Phaeton, the son of Helios.

Young Phaeton couldn't resist the urge to take those four fiery horses out for a spin, but he was an inexperienced driver and he lost control of the vehicle. Before a furious Zeus struck him dead with a thunderbolt as punishment, Phaeton scorched a big path in the sky. Today we call that path the Milky Way.

Magic Number 5

THE FIVE NYMPHS KNOWN AS the Heliades (daughters of Helios) were the sisters of Phaeton. After Phaeton's ride in the runaway chariot, Zeus struck him down with a thunderbolt. Phaeton fell to Earth, dead, by the banks of a river.

The sisters were so overwhelmed by grief they could not stop crying. They took root by the river, turning into poplar trees that shed tears of amber. (We'd call it sap.)

In Greek mythology, Charon was the ferryman who transported souls across the River Styx into the underworld. He was depicted as a crotchety old man who required a bit of bribery before he would do his job. So, in ancient Greece it was customary to bury someone with a coin in his mouth so he'd have the fare to pay Charon when he reached the afterlife.

CHARON IS THE NAME of the largest satellite (some people call it a moon) orbiting Pluto—once a planet, now reclassified as a dwarf planet, named for the Roman god of the underworld.

Even though Greeks and Romans had different names for the god of the underworld—Hades and Pluto, respectively—they both recognized Charon as the ferryman. He's even mentioned in Dante's *Inferno*.

Magic Number 5

RIVERS OF THE UNDERWORLD in Greek mythology:

Acheron
River of Woe

Cocytus
River of Lamentation

Lethe
River of Forgetfulness

Phlegethon
River of Fire

Styx
River of Hate

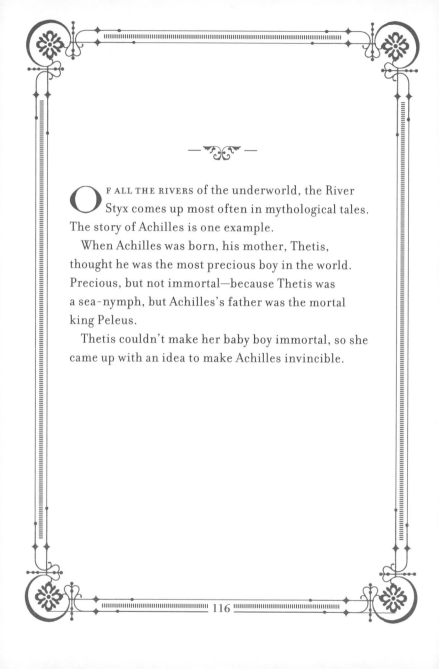

OF ALL THE RIVERS of the underworld, the River Styx comes up most often in mythological tales. The story of Achilles is one example.

When Achilles was born, his mother, Thetis, thought he was the most precious boy in the world. Precious, but not immortal—because Thetis was a sea-nymph, but Achilles's father was the mortal king Peleus.

Thetis couldn't make her baby boy immortal, so she came up with an idea to make Achilles invincible.

S HE CARRIED HIM to the underworld and dipped him in the River Styx knowing that the water would protect him from harm. But she miscalculated…

As she dipped him in the river, she held Achilles by one heel creating one spot on his body that the water couldn't touch. And that's where an arrow, shot by the warrior Paris and guided by the god Apollo, fatally wounded Achilles.

THE TALE OF ACHILLES gives us the expression "Achilles' heel" meaning a person's fatal weakness or vulnerability. Even a great hero like Achilles had a weak spot—just as Superman succumbs to the power of kryptonite—so we mere mortals can't expect anything better for ourselves.

—❦—

THERE REALLY IS A RIVER ACHERON in Greece. Plato wrote about it. The Roman poet Virgil wrote about it too. At certain places the River Acheron flows underground. Where could it possibly be heading? If you were an ancient, there was only one answer: Acheron was flowing directly to the underworld.

Real Places with Mythological Names

1. The Greek goddess of wisdom gave her name to...
   a. Albania   b. Athens   c. Minnesota

2. Rome was named for a boy saved by a...
   a. Bear   b. Lioness   c. Wolf

3. Based on the god for whom they're named, the Aeolian Islands might be...
   a. Sunny   b. Rainy   c. Windy

4. Nilus was the god of the River Nile. His daughter gave her name to what ancient Egyptian city?
   a. Cairo   b. Memphis   c. Thebes

5. What mythological daughter of the king of Egypt was ravished by the god of the sea?
   a. Libya   b. Morocco   c. Tunisia

ANSWERS

1. b. Ancient Greeks prized wisdom so it was only fitting that they named their most important city for Athena.

2. c. As babies, Romulus and his twin brother Remus were set adrift on the River Tiber. A wolf rescued them and cared for them.

3. c. Zeus gave Aeolus domain over the winds, which Aeolus kept in a cave in the Aeolian Islands near Sicily.

4. b. In Greek mythology, the daughter of the Nile was a freshwater nymph, or Naiad, named Memphis.

5. a. Libya was the daughter of Epaphus, king of Egypt. There are Greek and Roman myths about her rape by Poseidon (Neptune).

—❧—

IN EGYPTIAN MYTHOLOGY, the Phoenix was a magical firebird, associated with the sun. It lived for hundreds of years, and when it died it was reborn from its own ashes.

Who could resist such a fabulous creature? The ancient Greeks and Romans couldn't. They adopted the myth of the Phoenix into their mythologies. In the 19th century, the pioneers in Arizona adopted it for the name of their capital city.

How did the Aegean Sea get its name?

A summary of the long, sad tale: Aegeus, king of Athens, loved his son Theseus more than anything and Theseus loved him right back. Being a brave, strong young man, Theseus went on a mission to slay the Minotaur, which had been causing problems for Aegeus. Worried for his son, Aegeus made Theseus promise to have his crew raise white sails on the return voyage if he'd slain the Minotaur; black sails if Theseus was dead. Theseus forgot the promise, and returned with black sails on his ship. Seeing this and thinking Theseus was dead, Aegeus was so distraught he threw himself into the sea we now call the Aegean.

You might say that Atlas is all over the map. The Titan who holds up the heavens gave his name to the Atlantic Ocean, the Atlas Mountains in northern Africa, and the mythical lost continent of Atlantis.

And of course a bound collection of maps is also called an atlas.

— ❧ —

APHRODITE IS THE GREEK GODDESS of love and affection, but her name means "born from the foam" because she arose from the sea. As early as the 8th century BC the story of Aphrodite's birth on the Mediterranean island of Cyprus was recorded. The site of her birth is now considered to be a rock just off the coast near Paphos, where the waves crash together to create powerful white foam.

— ✦❧✦ —

THE BIRTH OF VENUS painted by Sandro Botticelli in 1486 is one of the most recognizable artworks in the world, but plenty of artists had depicted Aphrodite—or Venus—"on the half-shell" before Botticelli came along. An ancient Greek vessel in the collection of the National Archaeological Museum in Salonica, Italy, shows the birth of Aphrodite—cockle shell and all—depicted around 370 BC.

What's the difference between
Aphrodite and Venus?

The Greek goddess Aphrodite and the Roman goddess Venus both were the goddesses of love and beauty. But Aphrodite was a bit of a sexpot and she was known for encouraging infidelity and problematic relationships.

Venus was mellower and more nurturing; a patron of wives rather than mistresses.

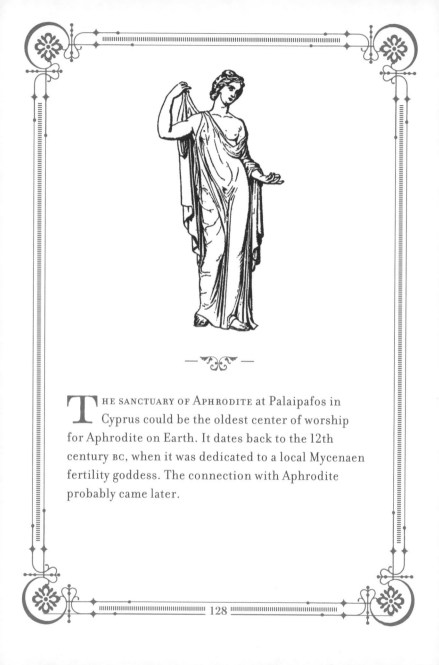

THE SANCTUARY OF APHRODITE at Palaipafos in Cyprus could be the oldest center of worship for Aphrodite on Earth. It dates back to the 12th century BC, when it was dedicated to a local Mycenaen fertility goddess. The connection with Aphrodite probably came later.

THE SANCTUARY OF APHRODITE at Amathous in Cyprus was associated with Palaipafos, although it was built much later—around the 8th century BC—and was part of a larger acropolis complex that, documents say, included a temple to Adonis and one to Hercules, although archaeologists are still searching for those buildings.

B ELOVED AS SHE WAS, Aphrodite had plenty of
weaknesses. For one thing, she was in love
with Ares, the god of war. (And you thought love and
war didn't mix!) Even though Aphrodite married
Hephaestus, the god of the forge, she cheated on him
with Ares.

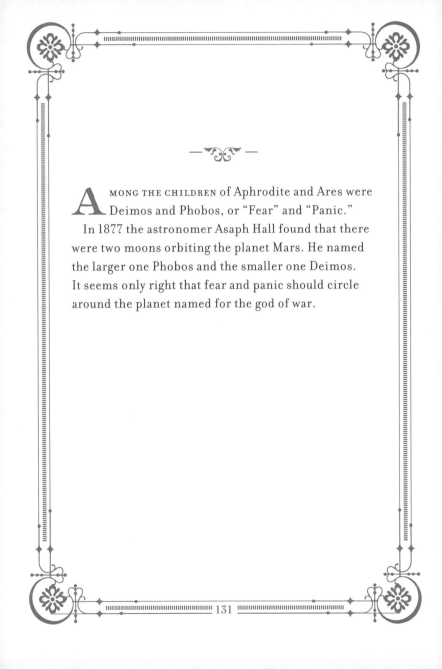

Among the children of Aphrodite and Ares were Deimos and Phobos, or "Fear" and "Panic."

In 1877 the astronomer Asaph Hall found that there were two moons orbiting the planet Mars. He named the larger one Phobos and the smaller one Deimos. It seems only right that fear and panic should circle around the planet named for the god of war.

Where does Eros fit into the picture?

The chubby little boy that the Greeks called Eros and the Romans called Cupid was Aphrodite's son—perpetually experiencing what parents know as the "terrible twos." He loved to misbehave, shooting his arrows wherever he chose—golden ones to incite love and leaden ones to quash it.

There are even statues and paintings showing Aphrodite about to spank Eros, but like most cute little "cherubs" he had his mom wrapped around his little finger.

POP QUIZ

Words of the Gods, Part II

1. An odyssey is a long...
   a. Journey   b. Book   c. Distance

2. A person under hypnosis can appear to be...
   a. Naked   b. Floating   c. Sleepy

3. An aphrodisiac is supposed to make someone...
   a. Amorous   b. Angry   c. Immortal

4. A mentor is a...
   a. Doctor   b. Teacher   c. Hunter

5. Narcissists are...
   a. Handsome   b. Conceited   c. Smart

ANSWERS

1. a. *The Odyssey* is the story of Odysseus, whose journey home after the Trojan Wars took ten years.

2. c. Hypnos is the Greek god of sleep. People under hypnosis look like they're sleepy, even though they're awake.

3. a. An aphrodisiac is a love potion. It's named for Aphrodite, goddess of love.

4. b. When Odysseus went to war, he asked his friend Mentor to be guardian and teacher for his son Telemachus.

5. b. Narcissus was very conceited and that caused him lots of trouble. Read on to learn how.

NARCISSISTIC PERSONALITY DISORDER (which most of us just call narcissism) is a psychological condition that causes someone to be completely preoccupied with himself—his looks, his activities, his needs, his importance, and what other people think of him. A narcissist is the type of person who never tires of looking at himself in the mirror. Just like Narcissus from Greek mythology.

N ARCISSUS WAS THE SON of the nymph Liriope and the River Cephissus (it's mythology...rivers can have sons) and he was so unbelievably handsome that everyone loved him—but no one loved Narcissus as much as he loved himself. He was so conceited that he treated all the people who loved him really horribly, until one of them asked the goddess Nemesis to punish Narcissus for being such a jerk.

N EMESIS, THE CHAMPION of spurned lovers, came up with a great punishment for Narcissus. She waited until he was wandering past a pool of cool, clear water. When he stopped to admire his reflection she made sure he became rooted to the spot where he stood until he simply couldn't tear himself away. And that's where Narcissus was doomed to spend the rest of eternity—gazing at his own reflection in a pool of water.

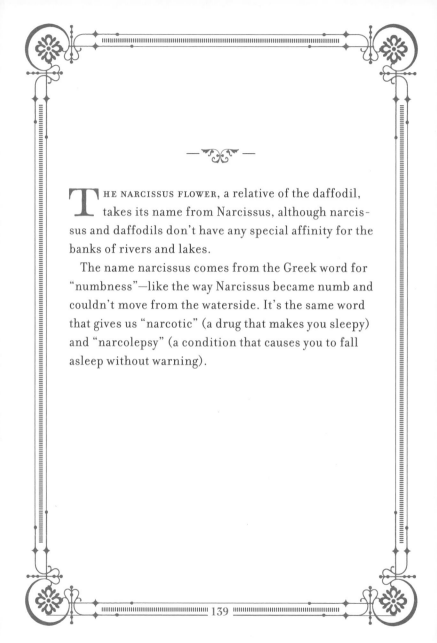

The narcissus flower, a relative of the daffodil, takes its name from Narcissus, although narcissus and daffodils don't have any special affinity for the banks of rivers and lakes.

The name narcissus comes from the Greek word for "numbness"—like the way Narcissus became numb and couldn't move from the waterside. It's the same word that gives us "narcotic" (a drug that makes you sleepy) and "narcolepsy" (a condition that causes you to fall asleep without warning).

WE CAN'T TALK ABOUT NARCISSUS without mentioning his little pal Echo. She loved him too, and—typical Narcissus—he did her wrong. But Echo wasn't a total innocent.

Long before she met Narcissus, the nymph Echo found herself on the wrong side of the goddess Hera. You can imagine how that turned out, but it's worth mentioning because the story reminds us of the perils of being a busybody.

HERA KNEW HER HUSBAND, Zeus, was playing around with other goddesses, nymphs, and assorted mythological beings. She was determined to catch him in the act, but Echo—who was known for being a blabbermouth—kept chattering away and warning Zeus every time his wife drew near.

Naturally, Hera didn't appreciate Echo's interference, so she doomed the little nymph to virtual silence. All Echo could do was repeat the last word someone spoke to her—and so became the origin of the eponymous term.

WHEN ECHO MET NARCISSUS she fell head over
heels in love with him, like everyone else
did. But Narcissus had no time for a little nymph who
could only repeat what other people said to her. So he
ignored Echo, and the more she chased him the more
he ignored her until finally she just faded away and
all that was left of Echo was a voice…voice…voice…
voice…

Words of the Gods, Medical Edition

1. A panacea is a remedy for...
   a. Death   b. All diseases   c. Frostbite

2. A phobia causes...
   a. Fear   b. Broken bones   c. Blindness

3. A syringe most closely resembles a...
   a. Star in the sky   b. Wave in the ocean   c. Hollow reed by a lake

4. Hygiene can keep you...
   a. Awake   b. Healthy   c. Warm

5. The drug morphine can lead to...
   a. Elaborate dreams   b. Hunger   c. Wrinkles

ANSWERS

1. b. Panacea, or Panakeia, is the daughter of Asclepius, the god of medicine. Her name means "cure all."

2. a. Phobos, the Greek god of fear, leaves his mark on people with irrational fears, better known as phobias.

3. c. Syrinx was a nymph who was being chased by the god Pan. To hide, she turned into a hollow reed by the side of a lake. A syringe is a hollow tube used to inject fluids into the body.

4. b. Hygieia, Roman goddess of health and cleanliness, was the daughter of Asclepius, god of medicine, and the sister of Panacea.

5. a. Morpheus, the Greek god of dreams, gave his name to morphine, which can cause people to become sleepy and to hallucinate.

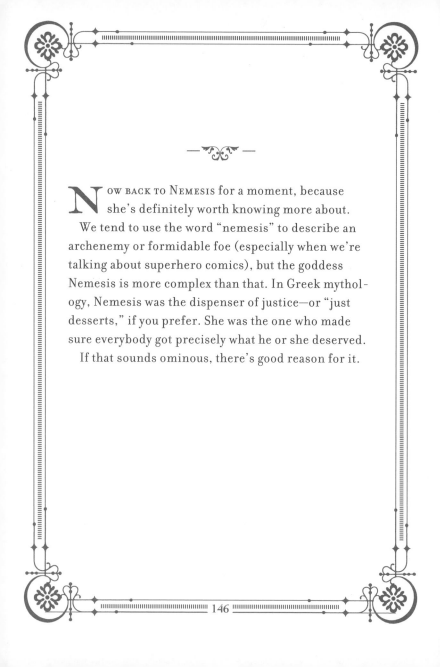

NOW BACK TO NEMESIS for a moment, because she's definitely worth knowing more about.

We tend to use the word "nemesis" to describe an archenemy or formidable foe (especially when we're talking about superhero comics), but the goddess Nemesis is more complex than that. In Greek mythology, Nemesis was the dispenser of justice—or "just desserts," if you prefer. She was the one who made sure everybody got precisely what he or she deserved.

If that sounds ominous, there's good reason for it.

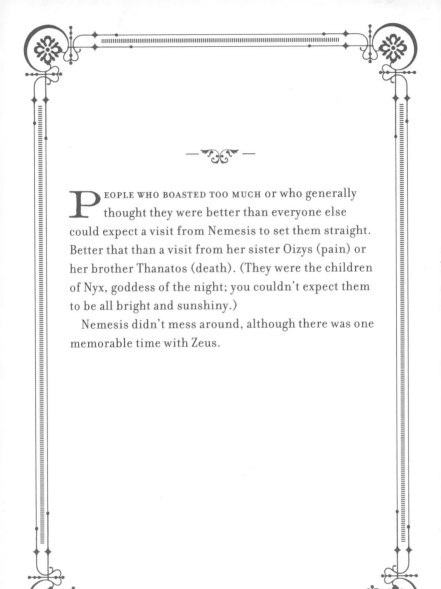

P EOPLE WHO BOASTED TOO MUCH or who generally thought they were better than everyone else could expect a visit from Nemesis to set them straight. Better that than a visit from her sister Oizys (pain) or her brother Thanatos (death). (They were the children of Nyx, goddess of the night; you couldn't expect them to be all bright and sunshiny.)

Nemesis didn't mess around, although there was one memorable time with Zeus.

Z EUS PURSUED NEMESIS relentlessly even though she made it clear she wasn't interested. (When have gods ever taken "no" for an answer?) She turned herself into all sorts of creatures trying to hide from him, but eventually—according to one story anyway— Zeus tracked her down while she was in the form of a goose and he a swan.

He had his way with her, and Nemesis gave birth to Helen, whom we know better as Helen of Troy.

A MORE COMMON STORY says that Helen hatched from an egg laid by Leda, and that Leda was the one Zeus pursued in the form of a swan.

Yet another story says that Nemesis laid the egg, but after it hatched Leda reared Helen as her own daughter.

It's always hard to pin down the definitive story in mythology.

Gods on Film, Part I

Ursula Andress: Aphrodite, *Clash of the Titans*

Sean Bean: Zeus, *Percy Jackson & the Olympians*

Roy Dotrice: Zeus, *Hercules: The Legendary Journeys*

Edie Falco: Artemis, *Gods Behaving Badly*

Chris Hemsworth: Thor, *Thor*

Tom Hiddleston: Loki, *Thor*

Anthony Hopkins: Odin, *Thor*

Liam Neeson: Zeus, *Clash of the Titans*

Laurence Olivier: Zeus, *Clash of the Titans*

Anthony Quinn:
Zeus, *Hercules: The Legendary Journeys*

Sharon Stone: Aphrodite, *Gods Behaving Badly*

Alexandra Tydings:
Aphrodite, *Xena: Warrior Princess* (TV series)

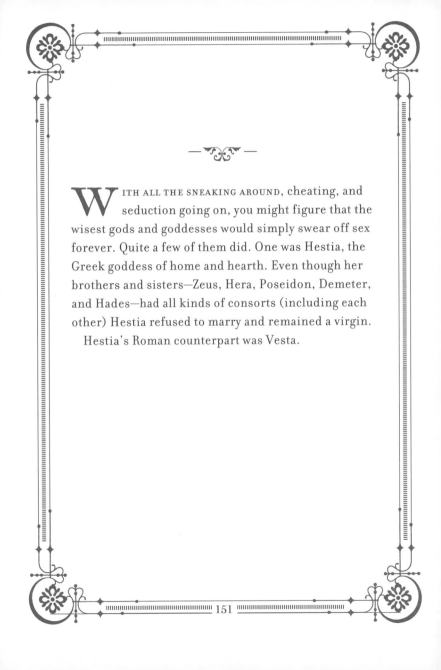

WITH ALL THE SNEAKING AROUND, cheating, and seduction going on, you might figure that the wisest gods and goddesses would simply swear off sex forever. Quite a few of them did. One was Hestia, the Greek goddess of home and hearth. Even though her brothers and sisters—Zeus, Hera, Poseidon, Demeter, and Hades—had all kinds of consorts (including each other) Hestia refused to marry and remained a virgin.

Hestia's Roman counterpart was Vesta.

Magic Number 6

— ❧ —

T HE PRIESTESSES WHO SERVED Vesta by keeping the ceremonial fires burning at her shrines were known as Vestales, or Vestal Virgins. Only six held these positions at any one time. They were chosen before the age of 10 and were required to uphold their duties for 30 years.

The Vestales held an important position in Roman society and were thought to possess certain mystical powers such as the ability to find runaway slaves.

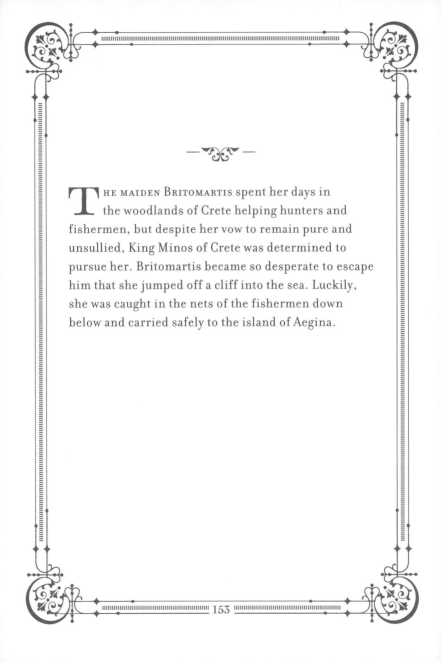

THE MAIDEN BRITOMARTIS spent her days in the woodlands of Crete helping hunters and fishermen, but despite her vow to remain pure and unsullied, King Minos of Crete was determined to pursue her. Britomartis became so desperate to escape him that she jumped off a cliff into the sea. Luckily, she was caught in the nets of the fishermen down below and carried safely to the island of Aegina.

— ✦ —

Artemis, Greek goddess of the hunt, was firmly committed to remaining chaste. Even a perceived threat to her modesty would place you in grave peril.

This brings us to the story of Actaeon…. He was an outdoorsy type and the grandson of Apollo, which made him the great nephew of Artemis—but even a family tie couldn't save him after he violated the goddess's most precious rule.

ONE DAY, POOR, FOOLISH ACTAEON was out wandering in the woods when he came upon a spring where Artemis and her handmaidens were bathing. Being the red-blooded deity he was, Actaeon stopped to admire the view. It wasn't every day that you spied Artemis in the nude—and there was a reason for that: she didn't want to be seen. What happened next is a warning to peepers everywhere…

WHEN SHE REALIZED what Actaeon had done (possibly because, like the dolt he was, he boasted about it later) Artemis turned him into a stag. But his troubles didn't stop there because Actaeon, you'll remember, was a hunter too and she traveled with a pack of hunting dogs—50 of them, according to the tale related by the Roman poet Ovid.

Those dogs recognized prey when they saw it. They took one look at that stag and tore it to pieces.

CLEARLY ARTEMIS TOOK HER VOW of chastity seriously. And if you were one of her chosen few, she expected you to be equally committed to preserving your purity. The nymph Callisto learned that lesson the hard way.

When Artemis heard that Callisto had been seduced by Zeus (yes, him again) and gave birth to a son, she was so furious she turned Callisto and the boy into bears. To make amends to Callisto, Zeus placed her and her son in the sky as the constellations we call Ursa Major and Ursa Minor—the Great Bear and the Little Bear.

*Did anyone ever try to put the
moves on Artemis?*

Orion did. And you can guess what happened to him.

Orion was a great hunter and some versions of this story say that he and Artemis (or Diana, her Roman counterpart) spent a lot of time together and became great friends. But the most common version of the tale says that when Orion tried to take their friendship to "the next level" Artemis became angry and shot him with an arrow.

Magic Number 7

THE PLEIADES, better known as the Seven Sisters, were the daughters of the Titan Atlas and the sea-nymph Pleione. They were:

Alkyone
Elektra
Kelaino
Maia
Merope
Sterope
Taygete

One story says that they were so beautiful the hunter Orion just wouldn't stay away from them. To keep them safe, Zeus placed them in the sky out of reach. Today, the constellation called Pleiades is among the easiest to identify in the night sky. Its nine brightest stars are named for the seven sisters and their parents.

Who's a Muse?

1. Ariadne	Yes	No
2. Calliope	Yes	No
3. Clio	Yes	No
4. Erato	Yes	No
5. Euterpe	Yes	No
6. Melpomene	Yes	No
7. Polyhymnia	Yes	No
8. Terpsichore	Yes	No
9. Thalia	Yes	No
10. Urania	Yes	No

ANSWERS

1. No: Ariadne is the wife of the wine god Dionysus.

2. Yes: Calliope is the muse of epic poetry and eloquence.

3. Yes: Clio is the muse of history.

4. Yes: Erato is the muse of love poetry.

5. Yes: Euterpe is the muse of music and joy.

6. Yes: Melpomene is the muse of tragedy.

7. Yes: Polyhymnia is the muse of religious hymns and she invented the lyre.

8. Yes: Terpsichore is the muse of dance.

9. Yes: Thalia is the muse of comedy.

10. Yes: Urania is the muse of astronomy.

No, really, who are the Muses?

The Muses were minor goddesses who governed artistry and provided inspiration for poets, painters, and other creative types. We get the words "music" and "museum" from muse. When we muse about something, it means we're thinking about it creatively. Models who appear in a painter's finest work or dancers who inspire great choreography are referred to as muses.

Ancient poetry often started by invoking the Muse—asking her to help make the writing beautiful. Dante, Chaucer, Shakespeare, and John Milton famously invoked the Muse in their works as well.

F EMALE FIGURES PLAY a powerful role in mythology and tend to possess the more admirable characteristics, from the gentle nymphs who protect the rivers and trees, to the nurturing Earth mother Demeter, to the fiercely loyal and self-sufficient huntress Artemis or her Roman counterpart Diana.

Athena, goddess of wisdom and the arts, was also the goddess of war and military strategy. So, when soldiers went to war, they prayed to Athena for strength, courage, and a swift victory in battle.

Why did soldiers pray to Athena
more than Ares?

Ares, the Greek god of war, was a bloodthirsty character who craved carnage. The Greeks accepted his role in the pantheon, but they didn't celebrate him. There are few statues or depictions of Ares from ancient times, and virtually no temples in his honor.

Mars, the Roman god of war, was a different character altogether. He was a warrior, but he also was a military strategist and a protector—much more like Athena than like Ares.

Weapons of the Gods

ANYONE CAN WIELD a sword and shield. Some mythological figures had more fantastic weapons at their disposal.

Aegis
Worn by Athena, this sacred goatskin
cloak provided protection from harm.

Gungnir
Odin's spear; it never misses its mark.

Mjölnir
Thor's magic hammer; it always
returns to his hand after it's thrown.

Poseidon's Trident
Made for him by the Cyclopes, it had
the power to create storms at sea.

Zeus's Thunderbolts
They could, kill, wound, or simply attract
attention; he had an infinite supply.

Warrior Women

Amazons
Society of female warriors, mentioned in *The Iliad*.

Bellona
Roman goddess of war, similar to the Greek goddess Enyo.

Camilla
In Roman mythology, a warrior virgin killed in battle.

Kyrene
Princess and huntress in Greek mythology.

Morrigan
Goddess of battle in Irish mythology.

Nike
Winged goddess of victory in Greek mythology.

Valkyries
In Norse mythology, they visit battlefields
and decide who lives and who dies.

—

K YRENE'S FAVORITE WEAPON was a javelin, but
she wasn't above hand-to-hand combat if
necessary. One tale says that to protect her father's
flocks from attack by a lion, she wrestled the beast
to the ground with her bare hands. Apollo saw her do
this, was totally smitten, and immediately carried off
Kyrene and had his way with her.

THE AMAZON RIVER in South America probably takes its name from the mythological race of women warriors. By some accounts, Don Francisco de Orellana, the 16th century Spanish explorer who "discovered" the Amazon, claimed he met up with the Amazons on his journey. (Who could contradict him?)

POP QUIZ

Crafted by Hephaestus: Treasure or Trouble

1. **Armor of Achilles**   Treasure   Trouble

2. **Necklace of Harmonia**   Treasure   Trouble

3. **Throne of Hera**   Treasure   Trouble

4. **Krater of Menelaus**   Treasure   Trouble

5. **Scepter of Agamemnon**   Treasure   Trouble

ANSWERS

1. Treasure: The armor Hephaestus crafted made Achilles nearly invincible.

2. Trouble: The necklace Hephaestus made for Harmonia, the daughter conceived when Aphrodite cheated on him with Ares, carried a curse that doomed her descendants.

3. Trouble: To punish Hera for tossing him out of Olympus when he was a baby, Hephaestus made her a golden throne with invisible bonds that closed around her as soon as she sat down.

4. Treasure: A krater is a type of bowl, and this one was crafted out of silver. King Menelaus presents it to Telemachus as a gift in *The Odyssey*.

5. Treasure: A scepter made by Hephaestus for Zeus was handed down through generations to King Agamemnon.

—❧❧❧—

Vulcan, the Roman god of fire and smoke, is similar to, but not the same as the Greek god Hephaestus.

Vulcan's fire is associated with the fire of a blacksmith's forge, so Vulcan is the god of metalworkers. He's also associated with fire that comes from deep inside the Earth. The word volcano comes from Vulcan. Scientists who study volcanoes are known as vulcanologists.

How did Vulcan become Mr. Spock's
home planet in Star Trek?

Mr. Spock comes from the fiery hot, dry planet Vulcan.
The name might have been inspired by an early astro-
nomical theory that there was a small, hot planet located
between the Sun and Mercury. Or *Star Trek* creator Gene
Rodenberry might have liked the Roman mythological
allusion: he named other planets in the *Star Trek* universe
Romulus and Remus.

In its definitions of Vulcan, the *Oxford English Dictionary*
includes the *Star Trek* planet and the race of beings who
live there.

Gods on Film, Part II

 OME OF THE ACTORS who have portrayed Hercules (Heracles) in the movies and on TV

Steve Byers
Immortals

Tate Donovan
Disney's Hercules (voice of the animated character)

Ryan Gosling
Young Hercules (TV series)

Dwayne Johnson
Hercules: The Thracian Wars

Arnold Schwarzenegger
Hercules in New York

Kevin Sorbo
Hercules: The Legendary Journeys (TV series)

Magic Number 12

H ERCULES (OR HERACLES as he was known to the Greeks) was a great mythological hero and the original "strongman" of mythology. He's best known for performing the so-called "Twelve Labors"—jobs that were so difficult no mere mortal could handle them. But he deserved his time of hard labor. The tasks were punishment for Hercules after he killed his wife and children in a fit of madness.

THE ELEVENTH LABOR of Hercules required him to capture the Golden Apples that Gaia, the Earth goddess, had given to Hera as a wedding present when she married Zeus. Those precious apples were guarded by the Hesperides, the "daughters of the evening," a trio of nymphs who were lovely and graceful, but perhaps not the most diligent guardians. Some stories say that they had the dragon, Ladon, watching over the apples, Hercules slew the dragon and captured the prize.

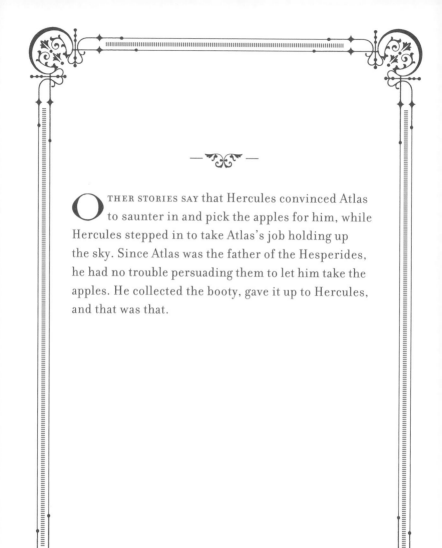

OTHER STORIES SAY that Hercules convinced Atlas to saunter in and pick the apples for him, while Hercules stepped in to take Atlas's job holding up the sky. Since Atlas was the father of the Hesperides, he had no trouble persuading them to let him take the apples. He collected the booty, gave it up to Hercules, and that was that.

—⚜—

THE GOLDEN APPLES of the Hesperides turn up
again at the marriage of Peleus and Thetis.
If you've ever coped with family strife at a wedding
you'll appreciate this story:

Thetis was a Nereid (sea nymph). Peleus was a war
hero. When they finally tied the knot, everyone was
invited to the wedding. Everyone except for Eris, the
goddess of discord.

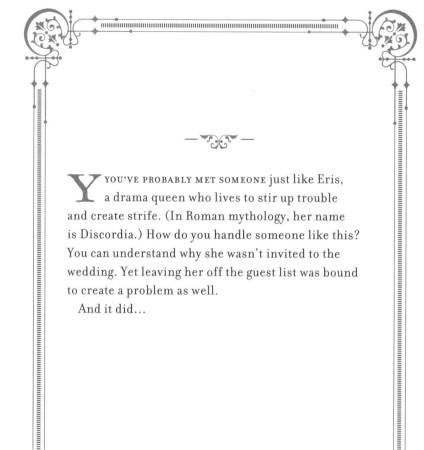

YYOU'VE PROBABLY MET SOMEONE just like Eris, a drama queen who lives to stir up trouble and create strife. (In Roman mythology, her name is Discordia.) How do you handle someone like this? You can understand why she wasn't invited to the wedding. Yet leaving her off the guest list was bound to create a problem as well.

And it did…

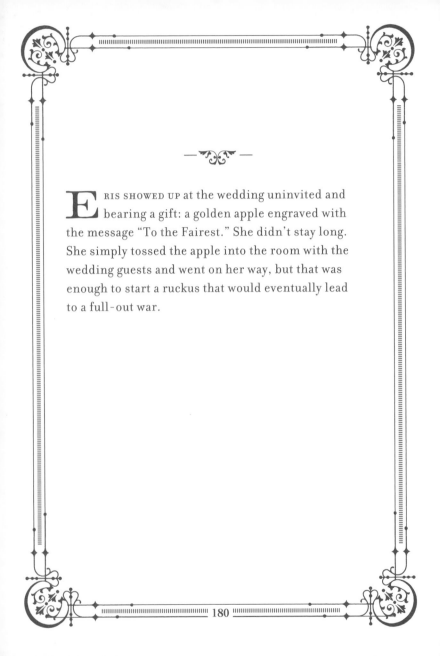

ERIS SHOWED UP at the wedding uninvited and bearing a gift: a golden apple engraved with the message "To the Fairest." She didn't stay long. She simply tossed the apple into the room with the wedding guests and went on her way, but that was enough to start a ruckus that would eventually lead to a full-out war.

I MAGINE A ROOM full of goddesses, each of whom has
an ego larger than life. Here's a gift addressed to
"the Fairest." Who is it for?

Hera picked up the apple, immediately figuring that
"the Fairest" meant her. But Aphrodite and Athena
were just as convinced the apple was intended for
them. The three goddesses broke up the wedding
celebration with their squabbling. They demanded
that Zeus decide who was the fairest of them all.

— ❧ ❧ ❦ —

WELL, ZEUS HAS HIS FLAWS, but he's no fool. He refused to make the decision and turned it over to Paris, a mortal prince whose father was king of Troy. But everyone has his price, and Aphrodite was able to bribe Paris into choosing her. In return, she promised to give Paris the most beautiful woman in the world—Helen. There was just one problem: Helen was already married to the king of Sparta. Paris kidnaps her. Helen's husband sends an army to Troy to bring her back. And before you can say "golden apple" the Trojan Wars have begun.

Children of Eris

Algos: Pain and Sorrow

Amphilogiai: Disputes

Androctasai: Manslaughter

Ate: Ruin or Folly

Dysnomia: Lawlessness

Horkos: Oaths and False Promises

Hysminai: Fights

Lethe: Forgetfulness

Limos: Famine

Makhai: Battles

Neikea: Arguments

Phonoi: Murder

Ponos: Grueling Work

Pseudologoi: Lies

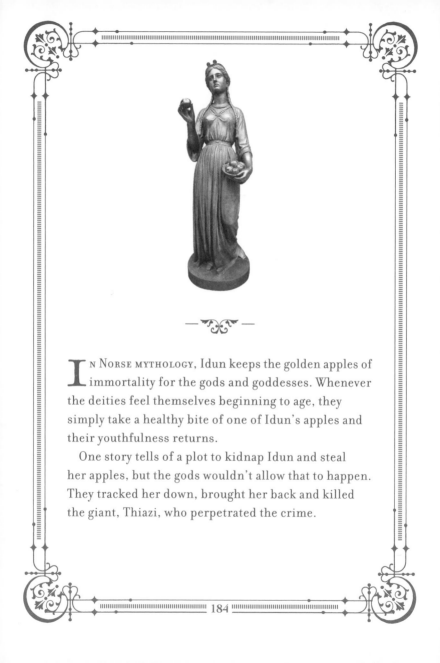

IN NORSE MYTHOLOGY, Idun keeps the golden apples of immortality for the gods and goddesses. Whenever the deities feel themselves beginning to age, they simply take a healthy bite of one of Idun's apples and their youthfulness returns.

One story tells of a plot to kidnap Idun and steal her apples, but the gods wouldn't allow that to happen. They tracked her down, brought her back and killed the giant, Thiazi, who perpetrated the crime.

G OLDEN APPLES also play an important part in the story of Atalanta.

Atalanta was a wilderness woman. Even though she was a princess of Arcadia, her parents abandoned her—because her father was disappointed that she wasn't a boy! They left her in the woods where she was suckled by a she-bear and raised by hunters. Like the goddess Artemis, she was an expert huntress and she was so strong and skilled she became the only woman permitted to join Jason's band of adventurers, the Argonauts.

LIKE THE GODDESS ARTEMIS (whom she idolized) Atalanta also vowed to remain chaste. But perhaps someone misheard her and thought she said "chased," because Atalanta—like any beautiful woman who also happens to be a princess and who swears off men—had a lot of men chasing after her. Literally. And that's where the golden apples come into the story.

—⚜—

ATALANTA'S EXPLOITS with the Argonauts and her role in slaying a dreaded beast known as the Calydonian Boar made her famous. So famous, in fact, that even her estranged father, the king of Arcadia, who had abandoned her when she was a baby, decided to get back in touch with her. And the first thing he did was demand that she find a man to marry.

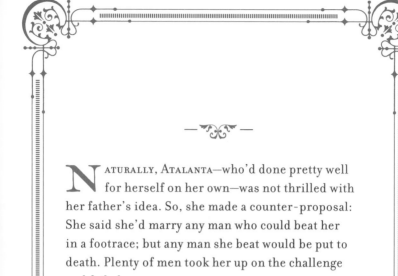

Naturally, Atalanta—who'd done pretty well for herself on her own—was not thrilled with her father's idea. So, she made a counter-proposal: She said she'd marry any man who could beat her in a footrace; but any man she beat would be put to death. Plenty of men took her up on the challenge and failed.

Then along came Melanion (sometimes known as Hippomenes). He knew he couldn't defeat Atalanta without divine intervention, so he asked the goddess of love, Aphrodite, for help. And Aphrodite's strategy basically involved distracting Atalanta with shiny things.

— ❧ —

SHE GAVE MELANION three golden apples and told him to drop them along the course during his race with Atalanta, which he did, and it worked. Atalanta stopped to pick up the golden apples and Melanion trotted past her to win the race.

Some versions of the story say that Atalanta slowed down on purpose because she wanted Melanion to win. Whether he tricked her into losing or she tricked him into winning, they wound up together, but their love affair did not have a happily-ever-after.

MELANION WAS SO THRILLED that he won the race, he neglected to adequately thank Aphrodite for her help. This, of course, was a big mistake. The goddess was so offended that she turned Melanion and Atalanta into lions, which might not seem too terrible until you consider that the ancient Greeks believed lions were incapable of mating with each other. (Good hunters though, for whatever that's worth.)

Notice the spelling of her name: Atalanta has no relation to the capital city of the state of Georgia. It's derived from the Greek word for "balance" and it translates to "equal in weight."

You could say that Atalanta was one of the first fighters for women's rights. Equal pay for equal work.

Magic Number 3

THE THREE FATES Clotho, Lakhesis, and Atropos were female deities who governed the events in a person's life—what we usually call his fate. Clotho was the spinner who started creating the thread of life as soon as someone was born. Lakhesis decided how long the thread would be. Atropos cut it off at the predestined point.

The word "cloth"—and related words, such as clothing—comes from Clotho, the Spinner.

— ❧ —

Y OU'D FIGURE RUNNING everyone's lives would
keep the Fates busy, but they still had time
for other pursuits. One myth credits the Fates with
inventing seven letters of the Greek alphabet—five
vowels and two consonants.

The warrior Palamedes invented the rest of the
letters and the god Hermes assigned each of them
a sound.

At least that's according to mythology.

Musical Weather Gods

Which deity suits the song title?

1. "You Are the Sunshine of My Life"
   a. Sol   b. Talos   c. Triptolemus

2. "Blowin' in the Wind"
   a. Eryx   b. Miletus   c. Zephyrus

3. "Raindrops Keep Falling on My Head"
   a. The Dryads   b. The Nephelai   c. The Spartoi

4. "Let It Snow! Let It Snow! Let It Snow!"
   a. Chione   b. Euryclea   c. Galatea

5. "Somewhere Over the Rainbow"
   a. Auge   b. Iris   c. Phoebe

ANSWERS

1. a. Sol is the Roman god of the sun, similar to the Greek god Helios. From Sol we get the word "solar," meaning "related to the sun."

2. c. Zephyrus is the Greek god of the west wind. In English, a zephyr is a gentle wind from the west.

3. b. The Nephelai are cloud nymphs. Their father Okeanos gives them the water they use to make rain.

4. a. Chione is the daughter of Boreas, the north wind, and Oreithyia, the cold mountain wind.

5. b. Iris is the Greek goddess of the rainbow. Her appearance in the sky meant the gods were sending a message to Earth.

IN HIS 5TH CENTURY BC comic play *The Clouds* (*Nephelai* in Greek) Aristophanes offers a humorous explanation for why the Nephelai are greater than Zeus himself: Zeus might be the god of the sky, but in order for there to be rain, the Nephelai must be present. ("Have you ever seen rain without clouds?" one character argues.)

As for the thunder that supposedly comes from Zeus: the character argues that it comes from the Nephelai, who fill up with water and bump into each other producing a crashing boom from the sky.

*Is that the only explanation for
thunder and lightning?*

No. Phenomena as enormous as thunder and lightning
had many explanations in mythology. Here's another:

Thunder and lightning were related to the three one-
eyed giants known as the Cyclopes. Brontes was the
"thunderer." (The dinosaur brontosaurus—"thunder
lizard"—takes its name from Brontes.) Steropes was
the "lightning maker" who forged Zeus's lightning bolts.
Arges was "flash" or "brightness," as in the stunning
flash of light that occurs when lightning cracks the sky.

I N Roman mythology, the Nephelai were known
as the Nebulae. From them we get the word
"nebula," a mass of stars resembling a cloud. They
also give us the word "nebulous," meaning indistinct,
misty or cloudy.

Magic Number 2

Harpies. You've met these squawking bird-women before. They represent the sort of irritating gust of wind that comes from out of nowhere and rips a paper out of your hand or the hat off your head.

The Harpies are usually depicted as a pair of ugly old hags with bird wings and talons for fingers, but sometimes they're pretty and sometimes there are three or four of them.

Everyone Knows They're Windy

Aeolus: Keeper of the winds

Apeliotes: Southeast Wind

Aurae: Nymphs of the Breezes

Boreas: North Wind

Eurus: East Wind

Kaikias: Northeast Wind

Lips: Southwest Wind

Notus: South Wind

Skyron: Northwest Wind

Zephyrus: West Wind

— ✦ —

As a group, the wind gods Boreas, Eurus, Notus, and Zephyrus are known as the Anemoi—or in Latin the Venti. The nymphs of the breezes—the Aurae—were sometimes thought to be the daughters of Boreas, the north wind and the most powerful of the four Anemoi.

If you're a weather watcher, you know that an anemometer is an instrument that measures wind speed. Guess where that name came from.

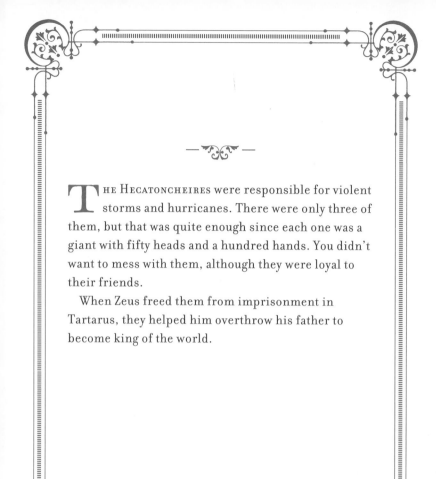

THE HECATONCHEIRES were responsible for violent storms and hurricanes. There were only three of them, but that was quite enough since each one was a giant with fifty heads and a hundred hands. You didn't want to mess with them, although they were loyal to their friends.

When Zeus freed them from imprisonment in Tartarus, they helped him overthrow his father to become king of the world.

THE STORM GIANT TYPHOEUS might be the most fearsome of all. He was said to be responsible for violent storms and natural occurrences such as earthquakes and volcanic eruptions. Some stories say he was so angry because he was trapped beneath the Earth inside Mount Etna.

Magic Number 2

THE ROMAN GOD JANUS was depicted with two faces—one looking forward and one looking back. He wasn't a major god, but soldiers had a special love for him because he could sense an enemy approaching from any direction and, in one tale, he even saved the city of Rome from attack.

The month of January, when we look back on the old year and forward to the new, takes its name from Janus.

The Days of the Week

I N ENGLISH, MONDAY IS NAMED for the Moon. Sunday is named for the Sun. And Saturday is named for the all-powerful Roman god Saturn. The rest of our days come from Norse mythology:

Tuesday: Tyr, god of wisdom, courage and glory.

Wednesday: Odin (or Woden), ruler of the gods.

Thursday: Thor, god of thunder, strength and protection.

Friday: Freya, goddess of love and fertility.

This just proves the names and stories and legacies of the gods are on the tips of our tongues every single day!

POP QUIZ

It's Not Always Friday

1. The Italian word for Monday is lunedì because it's named for the Roman...
   a. Goddess of the Moon   b. God of Work
   c. Goddess of Misfortune

2. In French, Tuesday is mardi, named for the...
   a. Goddess of the Hearth   b. God of War
   c. God of Thought and Reason

3. In Albanian, Wednesday is E mëkurë for the god of...
   a. Rain   b. Forests   c. Businessmen and Thieves

4. Thursday in Spanish is jueves, for the god of...
   a. The Sky   b. Sports and Games   c. Hospitality

5. Vineri is Friday in Romanian for the goddess of...
   a. Love   b. Wisdom   c. Sleep

ANSWERS

1. a. Luna, goddess of the moon, lends her name to lunedì, as Monday in English is named for the Moon.

2. b. Mars, the Roman god of war, is honored in the French word for Tuesday. If you tend to be in a fighting mood on Tuesday, maybe that's why.

3. c. In addition to being the messenger of the gods, Mercury watched over both businessmen and thieves.

4. a. Jupiter, the Roman god of the sky, was the principal deity in Roman mythology with powers similar to those of Zeus in Greek mythology.

5. a. Venus, the goddess of love, is celebrated in the Romanian word for Friday.